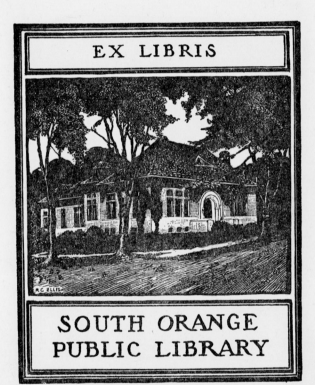

EX LIBRIS

SOUTH ORANGE
PUBLIC LIBRARY

JOHNSTOWN
the day the dam broke

By RICHARD O'CONNOR

J. B. LIPPINCOTT COMPANY
PHILADELPHIA • NEW YORK

Contents

JOHNSTOWN
the day the dam broke

1. The Storm Gathers

IN THE last two days of May, 1889, a great storm broke over the mountains of western Pennsylvania. A gentle, misty, springtime rain is rare in the high Alleghenies. When the thunderheads butt their roiling gray and black masses against the mountain walls, the collision produces a drenching for the earth below; the air seems to turn liquid; the rain pours down with a special malevolence. The earth quivers like a drumskin. Daylight turns a dark shade of violet. In the valleys deeply indented between mountain walls, where men and their works cling with an amazing persistence, the thunder and lightning are more than mere stage effects of the storm—they send down a cannonade that threatens annihilation. And when the storm passes it is like the lifting of a siege. This storm of May, 1889, came close to being a prolonged cloudburst.

It came from other mountains far to the west. The United States Signal Service, which performed the functions of today's U.S. Weather Bureau, traced it from birth in the central Rockies. On May 28 it began moving east through Kansas and Nebraska, entered the Ohio River valley and divided into two rain fronts. One low pressure area headed northeastward for New England, the other over the Alleghenies toward Virginia. On the night of May 29 the Signal

11

Service issued warnings of severe local storms throughout the Middle and South Atlantic states for the next day, Memorial Day. Right on schedule the skies opened up on May 30, dumping six to eight inches of rain over a 12,000-square-mile area of western Pennsylvania. The amount of water deposited on the western watershed of the Alleghenies by this storm has been estimated at 4,320,000,000 tons.

Western Pennsylvania really didn't need this additional soaking. For more than six weeks the mountains had been absorbing moisture in various forms. On April 6, a 14-inch snow had fallen and melted almost immediately. It rained on eight other days in the remainder of the month. The tempo of precipitation increased in May, with 11 days on which from one to six inches of rain fell, before the storm of May 30-31.

Draining off all this storm water greatly overburdened the rivers of western Pennsylvania. The Susquehanna and the Potomac, which drained the eastern watershed of the Alleghenies, flooded their banks in the effort to carry the rainwater off to Chesapeake Bay. The principal rivers draining the western watershed, the Allegheny and the Monongahela, were equally overburdened. Even more turbulent was the condition of their tributaries. Ordinarily graceful little brooks trickling down from the summits of the Alleghenies roared like millraces. Streams that flowed placidly through upland meadows in the summertime were torrents. The poetically named creeks, runs and branches tumbling down the shoulders of the Alleghenies and mirroring the placid scenes of a mountain summer became monsters of destruction tearing at farmlands, engulfing herds of cattle and snatching away bridges.

Three of the principal tributaries of the Allegheny are the Conemaugh River, Red Bank Creek and Clarion River. The headwaters of the Little Conemaugh are on the summit of a mountain ten miles east of the town of South Fork, where it receives the waters of South Fork Run. It flows down a deep valley to the confluence with the Stonycreek River, where the city of Johnstown is situated. Below this confluence it changes its name from the Little Conemaugh to the Conemaugh, flows swiftly for 25 miles before escaping the mountains through the Conemaugh Gap and merging with the Loyalhanna and the Blacklick in Westmoreland county to become the Kiskiminetas. The Kiskiminetas empties into the Allegheny, which flows into the Ohio, which joins the flood of the Mississippi. Thus the rain which falls on the summit of the Alleghenies, and flows down the western watershed, finally becomes a part of the Gulf of Mexico.

All through Cambria county course the streams with such homely and evocative names as Laurel Run . . . Paint Creek . . . Saltlick Creek . . . Trout Run . . . Shade Creek . . . Oven Run . . . Fallen Timber Run . . . Clapboard Run . . . Quemahoning Creek . . . Calendar Run . . . Spruce Creek . . .

The watercourses crisscrossing their countryside became more menacing by the hour.

Someone who left a pail out in the storm at the South Fork dam above Johnstown found eight inches of water at the bottom when the storm—and everything that came with it—had passed. Reports of damage in the region started coming into Pittsburgh and Philadelphia, principally through the Pennsylvania Railroad's communications, soon after the storm began May 30. The railroad itself was badly damaged; all divisions east of Pittsburgh reported bridges swept away, buildings destroyed, trackage undermined, telegraph lines down and locomotives and cars swamped. Up in the hills north and east of Johnstown was Cresson township, 2,300 feet above sea level, and it reported that streams which usually rose three inches in a rainstorm to about a foot of water, were running four feet deep, and a sunken turnpike had suddenly been flooded and itself was turned into a torrential waterway. At the town of Lilly, on the summit of the Alleghenies, Bear Run had gone berserk, knocked out a bridge and halted traffic on the Pennsylvania's main line between Pittsburgh and Philadelphia. Normally Bear Run trickled under the town through a culvert. Now the culvert was choked with tree branches and other debris and the water was running eight feet deep, flooding over the railroad tracks and forming a pond 25 to 40 feet deep around the railroad embankment.

These incidents were fair warning that the rivers of the western watershed would be reaching the flood stage downstream before long.

But Johnstown had learned to be nonchalant about floods; spring flooding was almost as inevitable as spring cleaning, taking a dose of sulphur and molasses, putting the long woolen underwear into mothballs. In the past two years Johnstown's streets had been flooded each spring during the heavy rains.

Since the first recorded flood of 1808, the town had been awash with the waters of the Little Conemaugh, the Stonycreek and their tributaries on more than a score of occasions. Almost every spring and occasionally in the fall the rivers would overflow their banks and force residents living along the river flats to move their furniture from the first to the second floor. There were even a few people around who remembered the "pumpkin flood" of 1820. That year the Stonycreek had gone on a rampage and carried thousands of pumpkins downstream to Johnstown from the upland farms. The whole settlement looked as though it had been bombarded with an autumn harvest. In 1847 a portion of

The Storm Gathers

the South Fork dam gave way and sent the waters of South Fork Run tumbling into the Little Conemaugh and then down on the city below. The borough of Conemaugh, where the Gautier wireworks were later to stand, was drowned in floodwater. The floods of 1859, 1862 and 1868 were also unusually severe. In 1887 and 1888 the springtime overflow caused a total of $100,000 in property damage.

Johnstown, industrious, prosperous and bustling almost from the day it was founded, adopted a phlegmatic attitude toward these afflictions. The disadvantages of living in a region where the rivers had a tendency toward seasonal tantrums, in the opinion of its leading citizens, were nothing compared to the natural resources which veined the countryside.

The city was founded in 1800 by a Swiss immigrant named Joseph Johns, who laid the town out on a 249-acre tract. At first it served mainly as a trading center for the farmers of the vicinity. The subsequent discovery of coal, iron ore and limestone made inevitable its development as a steel-manufacturing center. Johnstown did not really boom, however, until the development of the Bessemer steel-converting process. In the 1850s the town's principal industry, the Cambria Iron Company, ebbed to the point of bankruptcy and its creditors in Philadelphia were discussing the problem of whether to liquidate their losses or let the struggling company live a little longer. Daniel J. Morrell, the youthful member of a Philadelphia mercantile firm which was one of Cambria's leading creditors, then seized his opportunity. At a meeting of the firms which held most of Cambria's paper he pointed out that Johnstown's proximity to iron, coal, limestone and plentiful water power made it a natural steel-producing center, no matter what its temporary difficulties. The creditors rewarded Morrell's optimism by making him general manager of Cambria Iron and giving him a free hand to save the company any way he thought best.

In this position Morrell had to take chances or watch the company go under. He gambled on the tremendous growth of the country's industries and the amount of steel they would consume. The first 30-foot steel rails manufactured in the United States were rolled out at the plant in its main works below the confluence of the Stonycreek and the Little Conemaugh six years before the Civil War. The first Bessemer converter in America, a hollow, pear-shaped iron vessel still proudly exhibited in Johnstown, was set up at the Cambria plant in 1861. The Civil War, of course, gave further impetus to Cambria's production of rails, armor-plate, munitions and other requirements of a war in which the telegraph, the railroad, the armored vessel and breech-loading cannon were innovations.

In succeeding decades Cambria Iron grew to a size rivaling the Carnegie-Frick-Schwab empire in and around Pittsburgh, which was making the Krupps of Germany take respectful notice of the Pennsylvania steel magnates. Thus Johnstown itself expanded around the industrial complex of Cambria Iron and other foundries, blast furnaces and rolling mills.

Johnstown in 1889 was a borough of about 12,000 persons, with nine surrounding boroughs and several villages with a total of 18,000 population. The borough of Johnstown itself was not industrialized but housed the offices, shops, banks, theaters, print shops, churches and hotels of the locality, and the professional, mercantile and managerial classes had their homes on the slopes of the valley walls to which Johnstown clung. Social and financial position could be judged with great accuracy by the distance of a man's home above and beyond the river flats. The position of the other boroughs and villages in relation to Johnstown was as follows:

Cambria City, with its rows of tenements housing the ironworkers and their families, was just below the borough of Johnstown and the meeting of the Little Conemaugh and the Stonycreek. The Stonycreek flows generally northwestward from the hills of Somerset county, which adjoins Cambria county.

Across the Conemaugh from Cambria City was the Second Ward of the borough of Millville.

East of and adjacent to Johnstown was the borough of Conemaugh, where the Gautier wireworks were located.

Across the Little Conemaugh from Johnstown and Conemaugh were the boroughs of Millville, Prospect, Woodvale and East Conemaugh. The first three were largely populated by employes of Cambria Iron. The shops, yards and roundhouses of the Pennsylvania Railroad were in East Conemaugh.

Up the Stonycreek was the village of Moxham—actually large enough to be incorporated as a borough—where the Johnson Steel Street Rails Company was located.

The village of Morrellville, where many Cambria Iron employes also lived, was downstream from Johnstown on the Conemaugh, just above Sheridan Station and Coopersdale.

The borough of Franklin was situated up the Little Conemaugh, north from Johnstown and across the river from the borough of East Conemaugh.

Grubbtown and Roxbury were across the Stonycreek from Moxham and its rolling mills.

All these boroughs and villages were settled so deeply in the valleys of the Little Conemaugh and the Stonycreek that a visitor from the Middle West, accustomed to prairie

JOHNSTOWN
PENNSYLVANIA

19 miles to Conemaugh Gap

CONEMAUGH

Conemaugh

Little

Sang Hallow

East Conemaugh

Sheridan Station

Coopersdale

Woodvale

Fran

Morrelville

RIVER

P.R.R. MARSHALLING Y

PENNSYLVANIA R.R.

Millville

Cambria City

Prospect

Conemaugh

STONE BRIDGE

THE POINT

JOHNSTOW

Grubtown

Roxbury

Moxham

Ferndale

BALTIMORE AND OHIO

Stonycreek

River

Scale of miles

0   ½   1   2   3   4   5

8 miles to headwaters
of Little Conemaugh

River

PENNSYLVANIA R.R.

(PITTSBURG DIVISION)

South Fork

SOUTH FORK RUN

SOUTH FORK DAM

SOUTH FORK RESERVOIR

Sandy Run

N

W — E

S

JOHNSTOWN in 1889

Liam Dunne

Johnstown

vistas, commented in claustrophobiac horror, "Your sun rises at 10 A.M. and sets at 2 P.M.!"

"Johnstown was but the shopkeeper of the other boroughs," a New York *Sun* reporter wrote. "Millville lived on the payroll of the Cambria Works, as did the Borough of Cambria. Conemaugh lived on the payroll of the Gautier wireworks. Woodvale lived on the payroll of the Cambria Company's flour and woolen mills. And Johnstown in turn lived on them. It will thus be seen how one little group of Philadelphia money men controlled the valley. That these capitalists did not misuse their power is shown from the electoral returns of Cambria County, in which the majority was always Democratic, although the managers of the great iron plant firmly believed that the life of that industry and therefore that of the valley depended on the maintenance of a protective tariff."

Socially and commercially, he observed, Johnstown was vigorous and pleasure-loving. "It lived every moment. It swarmed with saloons. The place was accounted a good theater town by the profession. Sleighing in winter was a passion with the people, and after the first fall of snow the mountain roads about the town were musical with the tinkle of bells. There was not a boat in the often amphibious borough of Johnstown for the Conemaugh gallops like a race horse through the place, and for their boating the people went two miles up the more placid Stonycreek to Moxham, where there were skiffs, a park and free music furnished on Sunday by a band organized from employes of the Johnstown works [of Cambria Iron]."

Beneath the bright and busy surface, Johnstown was not entirely a happy place. The contrast between the lives of those who lived on the heights in their solid brick houses and those who were crowded into the tenement rows on the

river flats was too great for any widespread contentment.
The head of a household with a wife and five or six children,
rising before dawn, working 11 or 12 hours a day and six
days a week, and returning to a home with a minimum of
privacy, plumbing and heat, to which he brought a weekly
pay check of from $10 to $15 or less, was hardly living the
rich, full life. Generally speaking, the Anglo-Saxons dom-
inated the community socially and financially. The Germans, the Irish and the Scotch-Irish formed the overseer
and managerial classes in the mills and to some extent the
professional and mercantile classes in Johnstown.

As a whole, these people looked down on the strange,
garlicky swarm of "foreigners" and "immigrants" who
formed the laboring force in the mills and factories. The
newspapers usually referred to these people with delicate
inaccuracy as "Slavs." But they were commonly known by
less polite terms. The Hungarians were "Hunkies," the Poles
"Polacks," the Bohemians "Bohunks," the Italians "wops."
No exact epithet was found for the Czechs, Slovaks, Ser-
bians, Swiss and Austrians who were not so numerous. It
is only fair to say that the more lordly nationalities were also
known to each other in less than complimentary terms. The
Germans were "squareheads" or "krauts," the Irish were
"micks" or "paddies" or "bogtrotters," the Scottish were
"those—Orangemen." Nobody seemed to have thought of an
all-inclusive epithet for the Anglo-Saxons, perhaps out of
respect for their seniority among immigrants.

Johnstown was only a reflection of a national attitude.
The United States then was undergoing a periodic revulsion
against immigration and, contrary to the spirit of those wel-
coming words on the Statue of Liberty, there was a stinging
resentment of those who passed through Ellis Island without
a full set of 100-percent-American characteristics, presum-

Johnstown

ably acquired on the boat ride over. Before the Civil War, when the Irish and the Germans were entering by the hundreds of thousands, the Know-Nothings and the A.P.A. (American Protective Association) had risen to defend 100-percentism. Such yeasty movements subsided with the Civil War, when the ranks of the Union armies were filled only with the help of the recently despicable newcomers, but they came to life again in different guises to operate against other Johnny-come-latelys. These stresses and resentments were to burst violently to the surface in the days to come in Johnstown.

On such an occasion as Memorial Day, commemorating the dead of the Civil War which had ended 24 years before, these racial and religious embroilments were muted in an atmosphere of consecration, of devout recollection of the words Abraham Lincoln had spoken, over the mountains at Gettysburg. The North had stopped waving the bloody shirt, and the South was slowly emerging from its long preoccupation with the Lost Cause, but the war they had fought was still a part of living experience and the Grand Army of the Republic had not yet become a scattering of tobacco-stained old duffers exercising the rights of seniority on the benches of courthouse squares across the land.

That May 30 dawned with leaden skies.

The annual parade wasn't scheduled to move out until two o'clock that afternoon but the preparations for this modest display began early in the morning. The Union army veterans started gathering in the G.A.R. Hall on Main street at seven o'clock to visit the various cemeteries and decorate the graves of fallen comrades. Half an hour later the Sons of the Union Veterans formed up behind their drum corps and marched off to their annual ceremonies at the East Taylor cemetery. At 9:30 the delegation from Mineral Point arrived at the Pennsylvania Railroad depot with arms and wicker baskets full of flowers. The flowers were taken to the city marketplace at Main and Market streets where the Women's Relief Corps was making up bouquets and wreaths to decorate the graves, particularly those of Union veterans who had no one to remember them this day. It was a point of honor with the ladies of Johnstown that no soldier's grave lack flowers on Memorial Day. The women chatted gravely in the marketplace as they collected bouquets and wove wreaths from heaps of spring flowers, wild columbine, honeysuckle, snowballs, pansies, buttercups, piney buds, May apple blossoms. At one o'clock all business establishments closed their doors, and crowds began gathering along Main street. Out-of-towners were coming in on special trains, those from the east and west on the Pennsylvania, those from Somerset county on the Baltimore & Ohio.

The composition of the parade itself gives a fleeting picture of the times: the stout burgesses of the various boroughs, frock-coated, puffing along at the head of the procession; the Hussar Band, brave in scarlet tunics with gold frogging; the City Guard (Company H of the Pennsylvania National Guard); the Hornerstown Drum Corps; the Austrian Band and the Austrian Music Society; various fire companies with the brass fittings of their equipment shining; the Sons of the Union Veterans with their drum corps; disabled veterans riding in carriages; Odd Fellows and other lodge members in resplendent uniforms; the White Cross Society on foot and the ladies of the Relief Corps riding in carriages, and finally a hearse bearing a collection of muskets, bayonets and other weapons. The only uncouth touch to the whole procession, it was agreed, was the Union veteran in one of the carriages who insisted on waving his wooden leg at the crowds and offering various spectators a swig out of his bottle.

The parade proceeded up Main street to Adams and then out to the Sunnyvale cemetery, where wreaths were placed and a salute fired over the graves. The marchers then re-formed their ranks and proceeded back to town, the parade disbanding at Franklin and Washington streets, where the opera house was located, and the closing ceremonies of the day were held. Backstage the scene-shifters waited for the program to end so they could set the stage for the appearance that night of a touring company which was to present *Night Off*. The principal speaker was Colonel W. D. Moore of Pittsburgh. Most of the opera house's 900 seats were filled, and the audience was attentive, as always.

It was dark and drizzling when the program at the opera house came to a close and the people walked slowly home under their umbrellas. Over the splatter of the raindrops they could hear the roar of the two rivers rushing through the town.

Perhaps a few of the homebound people wondered if there was any sense of prophecy in Colonel Moore's oration, particularly when he said, "Peace has its dangers and battles, as well as war."

One of the few places in the city where Memorial Day had not caused a cessation of all activity was the Johnstown *Tribune* offices, on the floor over the post office, on Franklin street. In the local room, under the hiss and glare of the gas fixtures, reporters were scratching out their stories of the parade and other parts of the observance in longhand. A newspaper city room was a quieter place in those days before the teletype and typewriter and the two-way radio brought cacophony to the scene of editorial labors; there was only the sound of pencil gliding over paper, the faint, cricketlike chirruping of a telegraph key.

In his office off the local room George T. Swank, the white-haired and courtly editor of the *Tribune*, was meditating over reports of rising water on the Little Conemaugh and the Stonycreek and the fact that there was an even greater menace poised over Johnstown than the rivers themselves. That was the giant South Fork reservoir 14 miles above the town. If the dam impounding those waters ever broke, a monstrous catapult of water would descend on the city through the valley of the Little Conemaugh. Slowly and deliberately he continued writing his editorial for tomorrow's paper: "It is idle to speculate what would be the result if this tremendous body of water should be thrown into the already submerged valley of the Conemaugh . . ."

Idle? Perhaps. But a man couldn't help dwelling on the subject. Particularly on a night like this. Swank listened intently to the beat of the rain against the tin roof. It was coming down steadier now, and was expected to continue through the night and the next day.

In most of the city's homes that day's edition of the Johnstown *Tribune* was being read with an accustomed thoroughness by the men of Johnstown as they waited for supper to be placed on the table. A man still had his privileges in those days; he might be a dullard and an incompetent in his daily occupation, but when he got home he was the lord of the manor, entitled to and receiving respect, if not awe. One of his privileges was to read the evening paper while it was still in mint condition, before the women and children had at it.

The typical paterfamilias would not find any great or stirring events to engage his attention that evening.

Johnstown

From the "Local Notes" column he might learn that Professor Ferdinand Krogh's *Turnverein* pupils had been given a holiday; Oliver P. Ross had been appointed postmaster at Saxton; Justice John H. Fisher and his family were spending the day in Millwood, and the Quicksteps, the local baseball team, were "again defeated" in a game at McKeesport. There was livelier news under a Chicago dateline. A Dr. Cronin, whose disappearance two weeks ago had caused a considerable stir, was found dead in a sewer. The discovery of his body was quickly followed by the arrest of a horse thief, who admitted having committed the murder.

May thus far had not been a particularly juicy month for the inveterate newspaper reader. New York City was rather tepidly celebrating the 100th anniversary of George Washington's inauguration, the highlight of which was John Greenleaf Whittier's reading one of his poems. The lowlight, definitely, was the Centennial Ball, which a dispatch to the *Tribune* described as "a monument of incapacity and vulgarity." The dispatch added, with an almost audible titter, "Scenes in the supper rooms cannot be safely described in a newspaper." One day there was an account of how an "accident-proof" elevator was tested before a frock-coated assemblage of dignitaries in Providence, R.I., by hauling it up to the fifth-floor level of a building with three men, a basket of eggs and a glass of water in the cage, and then suddenly letting it drop. The experiment resulted in the death of one of the men and serious injury to the other two, in addition to which, all the eggs were broken and the water glass was shattered. The next day the death of Father Damien, the priest who ministered to the lepers of Molokai, was announced. In the middle of the month a New York court sentenced a man to the electric chair for the first time. Steve Brodie, the bridge-jumper, plunged into Passaic Falls and came out alive. Oklahoma had just been opened to settlement and federal troops had to be called to maintain order at Guthrie. And for the libidinous eye, there was a series of advertisements for Ball's corsets, "the corsets that need no breaking in."

So far 1889 had not given any promise of being a vintage year for spectacular news events or of being noteworthy in history. Suitably symbolic of the times was the man who had moved into the White House a few months before, Benjamin Harrison, who is vaguely remembered by all but professional historians as the good, gray and dullish fellow who was President between the two terms of Grover Cleveland, and perhaps as the grandson of William Henry Harrison ("Tippecanoe and Tyler Too"), briefly a resident of the White House himself. Yet Benjamin Harrison was not as colorless as he now seems; he had risked his hopes for the Presidency by strenuously opposing his fellow Republicans' Chinese Exclusion Bill. Nor was 1889 as placid, beneath the surface, as it seemed. Despite the belief that the frontier had been tamed for all time, an Indian prophet even then was rising in the West to preach the "ghost dance" religion, which held that Jesus Christ had been a false messiah and that an Indian savior would soon appear and drive the white man across the ocean. It would take a blaze of musketry at Wounded Knee the following year to convince the Indians that their theology had taken a wrong turn.

Even then Washington was swarming with the advocates of a greatly expanded, all-steel navy—not a few of them connected with the Pennsylvania mills where armor-plate was rolled out—which in less than ten years would help carry the nation toward its "manifest destiny" in the Caribbean, the Philippines and China. The army, also stirring out of senile dreams of the Civil War and the simpler days when guns fired one bullet at a time, was preparing to hold the first peacetime maneuvers in its history, out on the Kansas plains. The presiding officer was a Union cavalry general, and not unexpectedly the mock battle was a throwback to the good old days in northern Virginia. Scornful of aging generals, technology was perfecting the machine gun and other weapons to make a mockery of stately maneuvers on the battlefield.

But the Johnstown householder, rustling through the pages of his evening paper, found little to excite him the evening of May 30, 1889. The big news for him was the rain drumming at an increasing tempo on his roof.

2. The Dam Weakens

FOURTEEN MILES up the valley from Johnstown, South Fork Run empties its rush of mountain water into the Little Conemaugh. Almost two miles up South Fork Run from its mouth, on the night of May 30, 1889, stood the world's largest earthenwork dam. Its builders believed it to be impregnable. Judging from its dimensions and the engineering standards of the time, they had considerable justification for viewing their work with pride. It was doubtful, however, whether those engineers would have been quite so elated over their achievement on the night of May 30. The years had not been kind to the South Fork dam.

Even in comparison with today's monolithic steel and concrete dams, its proportions were considerable. It was 931 feet wide and 272 feet thick at the base. The rim of the dam was wide enough to accommodate a two-track wagon road. The structure rose more than 100 feet above the old creekbed to which it was anchored. Well made for the time in which it was built, the dam had a stone core extending 20 feet above the normal water line. It was filled with earth but reinforced with an outer wall of stone technically known as riprapping, which was 20 feet thick at the base and tapering to four feet thick at the top. A layer of slate was placed between the core and the riprap to hold the earth filling in solidly. Five 24-inch discharge pipes extended through the rock culvert in the base of the dam, the flow of excess water being regulated through valves operated from a nearby tower. A spillway 72 feet wide and ten feet deep was cut into the solid rock at the eastern end of the dam.

The dam stood 404 feet above the city—"our sword of Damocles," as some of Johnstown's citizens described it, not too seriously.

Behind its stout wall of earth and masonry were impounded the waters of South Fork Run and a dozen crystal-clear creeks and brooks running into the reservoir, or Lake Conemaugh as it was called. The lake was three miles long and more than a mile wide in places, the largest artificial lake in the country. Its bed was the bottom of an old ravine, and the water was 100 feet deep in places. Twenty million tons of water were impounded in the reservoir. That was the equation that worried some people in Johnstown for years: 20,000,000 tons of water, 404 feet above the city.

Many people felt as though they were living under a huge and rickety old wooden water tower which threatened to burst its seams at any moment. If the dam ever broke, they knew, it would be the equivalent of Niagara Falls pouring down the valley of the Little Conemaugh for thirty minutes.

It was for a canal that South Fork Run was originally dammed up, the waterway being a link in the fabulous transportation system which Pennsylvania built earlier in the century between Philadelphia and Pittsburgh. Early in the 1820s the state's leading citizens decided that it was much too wearisome to travel in stagecoaches over the Alleghenies from Philadelphia to Pittsburgh. A canal running all the way between the two cities was impracticable because of

The Dam Weakens

the intervening mountains. In 1824 the state began construction of an interlocking canal and rail system.

The first link was a horse-drawn railway between Philadelphia and Columbia, a distance of 81 miles; the second, a 173-mile stretch of waterways up the Susquehanna and Juniata valleys to Hollidaysburg. The celebrated Portage Railroad, one of the engineering marvels of the mid-nineteenth century, ran the 37 miles between Hollidaysburg and Johnstown. The rest of the journey to Pittsburgh, 105 miles, was water-borne. It took almost 36 hours to travel from Philadelphia to Pittsburgh.

Enthralled passengers on the water-and-rail system were conveyed all the way in canal boats. When they left the water, the boats were taken apart in detachable sections and hoisted on heavy trucks. They were reassembled when they left the rails to resume the journey by water. Thus passengers and cargo did not have to be transferred at each stage of the journey from boats to railway cars. Climbing the eastern slope of the Alleghenies from Hollidaysburg, the boat-sections were hauled up the mountainsides along inclined planes by means of stationary steam engines and heavy rope cables. Along level stretches of terrain they were hauled by horses. Later, locomotives replaced the horses because the teamsters who drove them proved too volatile in temperament for efficient railroading. Their brawling often delayed the trains. One of the features of travel between Philadelphia and Pittsburgh in the 1830s was watching a battle royal between teamsters inflamed by peach brandy available at three cents a tumbler.

Charles Dickens made the journey over the Portage Railroad and wrote glowingly of it in his otherwise disgruntled *American Notes*, published in 1842. "It was very pretty travelling thus at a rapid pace along the heights of the mountain in a keen wind, to look down into a valley full of light and softness; catching glimpses, through the treetops, of scattered cabins; children running to the doors; dogs bursting out to bark, whom we could see without hearing; terrified pigs scampering homeward; families sitting out in their crude gardens; cows gazing upward with a stupid indifference; men in their shirt sleeves, looking on at their unfinished houses, planning out tomorrow's work; and we riding onward, high above them, like a whirlwind." The scenery was splendid but the food, in the English novelist's opinion, was monotonous. He complained that at breakfast, dinner and supper they were served an unvarying menu of "tea, coffee, bread, butter, salmon, shad, liver, steak, potatoes, pickles, ham, chops, black pudding and sausages."

The South Fork dam was designed to provide the water for the canal from Johnstown to Pittsburgh, and $70,000 was appropriated by the Pennsylvania legislature for this purpose. A dozen years passed before the dam was finally completed. Just two years later, in 1854, the canal for which it was built became outmoded. In 1850 the state had started replacing the inclined planes on the Portage Railroad with locomotives, and four years later the whole system between Philadelphia and Pittsburgh was converted to a steam railroad. Horse cars, convertible canal boats, brawling teamsters, inclined planes and the canals themselves all became part of the picturesque past.

In 1857 the flourishing Pennsylvania Railroad took over the railway system, now that the pioneering and the backbreaking labor had been performed, buying it from the state for the bargain price of $7,500,000. The dam and reservoir on South Fork Run were included in the deal, not that the railroad had any particular use for such a white elephant among public works projects.

The Dam Weakens

The dam, in fact, was an unmitigated nuisance as far as the railroad was concerned. It seemed to have started deteriorating almost from the day it was finished; no wonder the state had offered it for sale three times between 1854 and 1857, with no bidders. Repairing it was an expensive proposition, and the legislature had been forced to appropriate $20,000 to mend the damage caused by high water in 1846, long before the dam was operative. The dam kept sprouting leaks, as water ate into the riprap and the earth filling it was designed to protect. In 1862 there was a more dramatic warning that the South Fork dam was not the soundest structure of its kind in the world. On July 26 that year a heavy rainfall caused the stone culvert under the dam to collapse and washed out a section of the dam wall 200 feet wide and 50 feet deep. The discharge pipes were opened to take the pressure off the crumbling wall, but no repairs were made by the current owner, the Pennsylvania Railroad, although the break left the dam greatly weakened, saddle-shaped in the middle—where it should have been strongest.

For years the dam simply moldered away up in the hills, visited only by hunters, fishers and nature-lovers, half forgotten in the city below.

In 1875, more than 20 years after it had been abandoned as part of the canal system, the dam and reservoir were purchased by Congressman John Reilly. He paid only $2,500 for it—a bargain, in a sense, since the state had poured a total of $190,000 into its construction and repair—but four years later Reilly sold it for $500 less than he had paid for it.

The new purchaser was Benjamin F. Ruff, who had definite plans for it. Isolated, set in a scene of rugged beauty, offering the perfect retreat for wealthy families jaded with city life and weary of inhaling the constant smoke fogs of

Johnstown

Pittsburgh, the reservoir would make a fine club site for people rich enough to afford it, Ruff believed. His vision, it turned out, was quite practical. The club was incorporated and sold memberships for $2,000.

The nabobs of Pittsburgh—the Mellon banking family, Andrew Carnegie and Henry Clay Frick—and such prominent citizens as A. V. Holmes, Philander C. Knox, W. L. Dun, John A. Harper and their families were eager to try the simple life up in the remote Alleghenies. Each family, as a condition of membership in the South Fork Fishing and Hunting Club, was privileged to spend two weeks at Lake Conemaugh in one of the cottages which lined the lake, or at the clubhouse near the dam. The membership was limited to 100 families, which made it even more exclusive—numerically—than New York's Four Hundred.

A local historian emphasized that summering on Lake Conemaugh was nothing like so pretentious and so opulent as summering at Newport, Tuxedo Park, Saratoga, Long Branch and other currently favored resorts of the wealthy. He wrote:

> There was no display at South Fork. The young men wore flannel shirts and crush hats, and the girls plain costumes that would not be injured in scrambling over rugged rocks or fishing in turbulent streams. There were a few modest cottages along the borders of the lake and a clubhouse. It was a comfortable home-like place and was as different from the ordinary fashionable summer resort as could well be conceived. The beautiful sheet of water bore upon its bosom in the soft evenings gay parties of young folks, some of whom would strum the mandolin or guitar . . . The club was a happy family party, and nothing more. There was an atmosphere of repose over South Fork Lake that it seemed nothing could disturb . . .

The Dam Weakens

It would be rather difficult to imagine Andrew Carnegie strumming a guitar by moonlight, the austere Frick scrambling over rugged rocks, or Andrew Mellon, the icy little man who became Secretary of the Treasury during the Republicans' long tenancy of the White House after World War I, paddling a canoe and doffing his wing collar for a flannel shirt. But perhaps in those days they had not calcified into the monumental figures remembered by later generations.

It was not until 1900 that Carnegie sold his interests in the Carnegie Steel Company to J. P. Morgan's combine for $487,556,160 and perhaps he still had a taste for the simple life. If so, it was his last fling at the pleasures of plain living. Shortly after the turn of the century he bought Skibo Castle in his native Scotland with its 28,000 acres, 40 guest suites, golf course, salmon run and deer preserves. Eight footmen were on the castle payroll with the solitary duty of pouring wine at table. There was also a staff bagpiper who awakened everyone for breakfast at 8 A.M., whether the hour suited him or not.

Even before he became the laird of Skibo Castle, Carnegie had a magnificent talent for scattering largesse. President Benjamin Harrison accepted a case of his favorite Scotch, "Queen's Vat" whisky, from Carnegie, and suffered politically when the gift was made public and he was widely criticized for letting a steel magnate buy his drinking whisky. Just to show he played no political favorites, Carnegie offered Grover Cleveland, a Democrat, a pension when he left the White House and was reported to be in financial straits. Cleveland declined with the proviso that "I might go to you when the fates are so hard with me that I must have a strong, friendly hand." Neither Harrison nor Cleveland could be credited with starting the practice of looking favorably upon patronage from the wealthy; during the presidency of General Grant, just about anything from a box of cigars to a Fifth Avenue mansion could be delivered at the back door of the White House.

The Carnegies, the Fricks and the Mellons were still on the best of terms in those days of summering at Conemaugh Lake. Andrew Mellon's father, Thomas, while still a minor figure in Pittsburgh banking, had provided the financial support for Frick's ambitions to take over the coke industry of Pennsylvania when he was only 21 years old. Carnegie, too, appreciated Frick's tempered-steel determination to dominate whatever field he chose, and made him a Carnegie partner. In the subsequent Homestead strike Frick demonstrated that Mellon and Carnegie had not overestimated the case-hardened qualities of their protégé. Frick ran in hundreds of Pinkerton men and private armed guards, and five months of slaughter on both sides followed. Public sentiment was running strong against Frick and his associates when an anarchist named Alexander Berkman made the tactical error of trying to kill Frick and thus swayed public opinion toward the steel magnates.

The bonds of affection and mutual financial interest between Carnegie and Frick broke in 1900 when Carnegie tried to ease Frick out of Carnegie Steel by buying Frick's shares at their book value of $4,900,000 just before Carnegie sold out to J. P. Morgan. Frick well knew that their actual value was $15,000,000. He became so enraged that, according to Philander C. Knox, an eyewitness, he chased his old patron out of his office on the ninth floor of the Carnegie Building in Pittsburgh and down the corridor before the agile Carnegie outran him. Knox, a fellow member of the South Fork Fishing and Hunting Club, a onetime United States Senator, Attorney General and Secretary of State, described the scene: "The white whiskers of the Scotch iron-master sang like the needles of a music box in the breeze made by Carnegie's energy in seeking a place where Frick was not."

Despite the presence of these personages from Pittsburgh on the South Fork Fishing and Hunting Club's roster, Johnstown was not overwhelmed with joy when the club took over the South Fork reservoir. The club soon made it plain that, for all the wealth of its membership, there was no intention of making thorough repairs on the dam. The discharge pipes were broken and inoperative. Nor could excess water be drained around the dam, for the spillway was fitted with gates to prevent the game fish with which the lake was stocked from escaping. The break incurred by the floods of 1862 was repaired haphazardly after the club assumed ownership of the reservoir; it was filled in with tree stumps, sand, clay, hemlock branches, straw and leaves—whatever seemed to be at hand. The club members were more concerned with their bass and pickerel than the dam which enclosed their lake. They regarded the dam as someone else's responsibility. Just because they had bought the lake didn't mean they had to put out good money to repair a dam built a good many years before by the state, did it? Laissez-faire was their battle cry in business, down in Pittsburgh, and it served them nicely in their summer retreat in the hills above Johnstown.

In the light of what happened on May 31, 1889, certain correspondence between Daniel J. Morrell, president and general manager of the Cambria Iron Company, and Benjamin F. Ruff, then the president of the South Fork Fishing and Hunting Club, which took place in 1880, has a rather morbid significance, although it did not result in any effective steps to bolster the dam.

Johnstown

Cyrus Elder, general counsel for Cambria Iron, later disclosed Morrell's concern over the dam. If it ever collapsed and flooded the Conemaugh valley, Cambria Iron would be the heaviest financial sufferer, with $50,000,000 invested in and around Johnstown. "When the South Fork Fishing and Hunting Club leased the lake and proposed to rebuild the old dam the Cambria Iron Company was considerably exercised and a competent engineer was employed to inspect the old dam and the plans for the reconstruction," Elder later told a New York *Sun* reporter. "My son George was at the Troy Polytechnic Institute at the time, and he sent to me a copy of a problem submitted to his class by the professor. It was a hypothetical case but was quite evidently based on the plans and specifications for the South Fork dam. The class decided the dam was safe. But the president of my company was still anxious and, thinking it would be a good idea to have some member of the company inside the South Fork Fishing and Hunting Club, set aside funds of the company for the purchase of two shares in the club."

The "competent engineer" mentioned by Cyrus Elder was John Fulton, who made a thorough inspection of the lake and dam site with his assistant, W. A. Fellows; Colonel E. J. Unger and C. A. Carpenter, members of the club, and W. M. McDowell, a Pittsburgh engineer. Fulton submitted his report to Morrell on November 26, 1880. It read in part:

There appear to me two serious elements of danger in the dam: First, the want of a discharge pipe to reduce or take the water out of the dam for needed repairs. Second, the unsubstantial method of repair, leaving a large leak which appears to be cutting the new embankment.

As the water cannot be lowered, the difficulty arises of reaching the course of the present destructive leaks. At present there is 40 feet of water in the dam. When the full head of 60 feet is reached it appears to me to be only a question of time until the former cutting is repeated.

Should this break be made during a season of flood, it is evident that considerable damage would ensue along the line of the Conemaugh. It is impossible to estimate how disastrous this flood would be, as its force would depend on the size of the breach in the dam with proportional rapidity of discharge.

The stability of the dam can only be measured by a thorough overhauling of the present lining on the upper slope and the construction of an ample discharge pipe to reduce or remove the water to make necessary repairs.

Morrell forwarded a copy of Fulton's report to Ruff, but the latter evidently was quite unimpressed. He replied that in the club's opinion the dam had been adequately repaired and concluded by stating, "You and your people are in no danger from our enterprise."

Not at all satisfied by this assurance, Morrell had the Pennsylvania Railroad—as the second most interested party concerned with the financial consequences of a possible break in the dam and a major disaster in the industrialized valley below it—assign two of its engineers to inspect the dam. The two experts disagreed between themselves and submitted conflicting reports on their findings.

Morrell may or may not have been troubled by presentiments of disaster—probably not, being a hardheaded man of business with little trust in premonition—but the unadorned facts of the situation were alarming enough to keep nagging at him—at least during the year 1880.

Again he wrote Ruff, still in a conciliatory mood:

We do not wish to put any obstruction in the way of your accomplishing your object in the reconstruction of the dam; but we must protest against the erection of a dam at that place, that will be a perpetual menace to the lives and property of those residing in the upper valley of the Conemaugh from its insecure construction. [In referring to the "reconstruction" and "erection" of the South Fork dam, Morrell actually meant the repairs contemplated or in the process of being completed.]

In my judgment there should have been provided some means by which the water could be let out of the dam in case of trouble, and I think that you will find it necessary to provide an outlet pipe or gate before any engineer could pronounce the job a safe one.

If this dam could be securely reconstructed with a safe means of driving off the water in case any weakness manifests itself, I should regard the accomplishment of this work a very desirable one, and if some arrangement could be made with your association by which the store of water in this reservoir could be used in time of great drouth in the mountains, this company would be willing to cooperate with you in the work and contribute liberally toward making the dam absolutely safe.

But the South Fork Hunting and Fishing Club wanted no interference with its affairs, no matter how nicely proposed or kindly intended. The club was convinced that a patchwork of mud, straw and hemlock branches sufficed to repair the weakness in the South Fork dam, and did not propose to have outsiders invading their much-cherished privacy. Its confidence in the soundness of the dam was not entirely shared by the people of the neighborhood. A Cambria county mine owner who had property near the dam requested that his own engineer inspect the reservoir frequently. He subsequently told newspapermen, with a request that his name be withheld, that he went to the sheriff of Cambria county and informed him it was "his duty to apply for an injunction" against the club, requiring either that the dam be torn down or reconstructed sufficiently to guarantee the safety of the valley below. Instead of going to court, the sheriff consulted Cambria Iron officials, the mine owner recalled, and the matter was dropped.

J. B. Montgomery, a railroad contractor, inspected the dam after it was included in the Pennsylvania Railroad's purchase of the canal and rail system between Philadelphia and Pittsburgh. "I have heard it said that the waste gates had not been opened for a great many years," Montgomery commented. "If this is so, no wonder the dam was rotten. Naturally the fishermen did not want to open the gates after the lake was stocked, for the fish would have run out. When the water reached a certain height there should have been a way of allowing it to escape. The dam was not built with the intention that the water should flow over the top of it under any circumstances, and if allowed to escape in that way the water was bound to undermine it in a short time. With a dam of this height, the pressure of a quantity of water great enough to overflow it must have been something tremendous."

With the wisdom of hindsight, the New York *Engineering News* later published the results of its survey:

> No engineer of known and good standing could possibly have been engaged in the reconstruction of the old dam after it had been neglected in disuse for twenty-odd years, and the old dam was a very inferior piece of work, of a kind wholly unwarranted by good engineering practices of its day, thirty years ago. [Most experts, however, even with the advantage of hindsight, agreed that the dam was fairly well constructed for its time and could have been safely shored up with the expenditure of much more money and labor.] Both the original dam and the reconstructed one were built of earth only, with no heart wall and riprapped only on

the slopes. True, the earth is of a sticky, clayey quality; the best of earth for adhesiveness, and the old dam was made in watered layers, well rammed down . . . But the new end probably was not rammed at all; the earth was simply dumped in like an ordinary railroad filling.

It has been an acknowledged principle of dam construction for forty years to build a central wall of puddle or solid masonry, but there was neither in the old nor the new dam. It is doubtful if there is another dam of the height of fifty feet in the United States which lacks this central wall. [Actually the South Fork dam had a stone core rising 20 feet above the "normal" water line.]

Ignorance or carelessness is shown in the reconstruction, for the middle of the new dam was nearly two feet lower than at the ends. It should have been crowned in the middle by all the rules and practices of engineering.

Had the break begun at the ends, the cut of the water would have been gradual and little or no harm would have resulted.

Negligence in the mere execution of the earthwork, however, if it existed, is of minor importance, since there is no doubt that it was not a primary cause of the trouble; at worst, it merely exaggerated it. The primary causes were the lowering of the crest, the dishing, or central sag in the crest, the closing of the bottom culvert, and the obstruction of the spillway.

Generally, it was agreed by the experts who studied the dam that there should have been spillways at both ends of it, instead of only on the eastern side; two spillways might have been able to carry off enough water to prevent the tremendous build-up of pressure against the center of the dam. The experts also agreed that the discharge pipes in the stone culvert at the base of the dam should have been opened and kept open, regardless of the bass and pickerel that might have escaped to more plebeian waters below. Particularly dangerous—the experts were unanimous on this point—was the fact that the dam was sway-backed. When the heavy rain began falling the night of May 30th, and the excess water began spilling over the center, the pressure of all 20,000,000 tons (or four and a half billion gallons) in the lake was concentrated against the middle of the dam.

. . . On the night of May 30 at Conemaugh Lake there was no hint of summer pleasures, no strumming of mandolins or girlish laughter. It was too early for the summer group of the South Fork Fishing and Hunting Club members, too late for those belonging to the hunting set. The only sounds were the lonely music the wind made in the pines, the percussive effects of the rain beating on the lake, and the rush of the feeders pouring down from the mountains. The cabins around the lake's edge were dark and empty. The lake's modest fleet, which participated in a regatta at the climax of the season, was secured to its docks, including two steam yachts, four sailboats, 50 canoes and rowboats.

In the three-story, wooden clubhouse near the dam site three worried men sat in conference, Colonel E. J. Unger, president of the club; W. Y. Boyer, superintendent of the grounds, and John G. Parke, the newly appointed resident engineer. Near by, under tents, were 75 workmen who had been digging sewer trenches from the cabins to an outlet below the dam. The club members had long been accustomed to the luxury of indoor plumbing down in Pittsburgh, and had decided that roughing it at Lake Conemaugh need not necessarily involve trotting off to outdoor privies in the middle of the night.

Unger, Boyer and Parke were reluctant to admit their apprehension to one another. Of them all, Parke felt the heaviest burden of responsibility. He was a 23-year-old Philadelphian, a rather pale and intense young man; this was his first job and he meant to make good at it. Parke was the favorite nephew of one of the U.S. Army Corps of Engineers' top officers, Major General John G. Parke, then about to retire as superintendent of West Point. His uncle-namesake, who had no son of his own and looked upon his nephew as a sort of filial substitute, had served as General Burnside's chief of staff at South Mountain, Antietam and Fredericksburg. In the campaign against Vicksburg, General Parke commanded the IX Corps under Grant. Parke then reverted to the rather inept command of General Burnside for the campaigns in the Wilderness and before Petersburg. His reputation survived the constant blundering of his chief. Subsequently, during the absence of General Meade, Parke commanded the Army of the Potomac in the field. So the younger Parke was determined to live up to an honored name. The declaration of Colonel Moore in his Memorial Day address that day, that peace has its heroes as well as war, applied very well, it developed, to young Parke.

. . . Even more obsessed with the possibility that something disastrous would happen to the South Fork dam was a dour little man standing on the shore of the lake. He was Herbert Webber, who had been employed by the club almost since it was organized as a guard on its hunting preserves and a caretaker for the cottages. In return he received a small wage, the right to hunt in its woods, and a one-room hut far up the lake and away from the cottages of the club members.

The condition of the dam had long been an obsession with Webber. He was an unsociable man, who placed no great value on human companionship, but it didn't seem right to him that a dam with three miles of lake behind it should endanger the city below—even if he had no use for the city himself.

Later he told newspapermen about his thoughts of that evening as he stood at the lake's edge and watched the water creeping up the shore line. He remembered calling the attention of the club's members to the faulty state of the dam and being told "it was built to last centuries." He also remembered that when he continued his warnings, making something of a gadfly of himself when the members wanted to enjoy themselves and leave their worries behind in Pittsburgh, he was told, "Shut up or you'll be bounced."

Webber, earlier that spring, had carried his forebodings to Johnstown city officials and warned them that the dam would give way if there was a heavy rainfall that spring. He was assured that an expert employed by the city would examine the dam and, if his conclusions agreed with Webber's, an appeal would be made to the state government at Harrisburg for help in repairing the dam or requiring the club to do so.

Nothing had happened in regard to his warnings.

For the past three days, he later told the press, he had watched water spouting from the dam as if it were a "giant watering pot." But nothing was being done. The ditch-diggers up until darkness that day had been kept at the job of providing indoor plumbing for the cabins; those 75 men should have been doing something about those leaks. Webber knew that the bosses conferring in the clubhouse were pinning their hopes on a quick end to the rainstorm. They ought to be on their knees, praying, Webber thought. It would take a miracle to stop this storm. You could smell it in the air: a long, steady downpour.

All night the rain kept falling over the Alleghenies, swelling the mountain lake so that it bulged at the seams of the earthen wall which contained it. Four hundred and four feet below, 14 miles away, the ten boroughs of Johnstown were sleeping—their last peaceful sleep for many months.

3. The Town Moves Upstairs

IN JOHNSTOWN the next morning Friday, May 31, the prospects were rather grim. The rain which had begun falling the previous afternoon had increased from a steady downpour to an unrelieved deluge about eleven o'clock the night before. There was no sign of a letup. The rivers were already overflowing their banks and flooding the lower parts of town. All this, of course, was expected, following the torrential rains of that spring. Much of the city was situated in the apex of the triangle formed by the confluence of the Little Conemaugh and the Stonycreek. In addition, the channels in which the rivers flowed through Johnstown were exceedingly narrow and forced the water higher. The Johnstown *Tribune* had observed during the previous year's spring flood that "A two-inch stream cannot be forced through a one-inch pipe." At their juncture, too, the rivers met and clashed with a great upsurge of water, which washed back over the low-lying streets. The triangular part of the city between the two rivers was caught in a sort of hydraulic nutcracker.

That the dam which contained the South Fork reservoir, or Conemaugh Lake, might some day break was generally pushed into the back of people's minds. There was nothing else to do, except move away. They could find some consolation in the fact that the Cambria Iron Company and the Pennsylvania Railroad, the two biggest property owners in the valley of the Little Conemaugh, were "in the same boat"; that their engineers presumably were keeping a periodic watch on the condition of the dam, and that the wealthy gentlemen who owned the lake were correct in saying that the dam was sound. They could also comfort themselves with the thought that nothing disastrous had happened yet, and probably wouldn't in their lifetimes. People have a way of deferring calamity to succeeding generations.

Victor Heiser, who became celebrated as a plague fighter and U.S. Public Health Service official around the fever spots of the world, was a 16-year-old boy living in Johnstown at the time. In his autobiography, *An American Doctor's Odyssey* (New York, 1936), he described the attitude of his fellow citizens: "The townspeople, like those who live in the shadow of Vesuvius, grew calloused to the possibility of danger. 'Some time,' they thought, 'that dam will give way, but it won't ever happen to us.'"

The journalistic profession, with its natural tendency to "view with alarm," had been anything but alarmed over the possibility of a disastrous break in the South Fork dam. After the high water of 1887, the Johnstown *Tribune* assured its readers that there was no danger of trouble in that direction unless the dam was breached simultaneously with a severe flood on the Little Conemaugh, "which," the editorial writer blithely concluded, "is one of the possibilities not worth worrying about."

The matter of the dam's safety had often come up before the city council of Johnstown, of course, but it was a desultory debate that continued over the years. The council had no actual jurisdiction over the dam, 14 miles above the town; it could only suggest, advise or plead that the owners take good care that the reservoir stay in its place. Had it been completely aroused over the danger, however, the council could have raised such a storm of protest that the South Fork Fishing and Hunting Club would have been forced to take remedial action. But it was 1889, and wealth had its inalienable privileges. It was regarded with a silent awe.

Yet it would be unfair to suggest that the whole town was somnolent, unaware of the danger that threatened from the tree-bordered reservoir above Johnstown. Enough people had gone picnicking below the dam—they were not permitted on the club's property, of course—or had been attracted to the place by curiosity or fear, to comprehend that the dam was a rickety structure of mud, straw and stone. They could see for themselves that it looked like the wall of a gigantic, not particularly house-proud bird's nest, rather than the bulwark which held back 20,000,000 tons of water. A longtime resident of Johnstown who, apparently still mindful of the power and glory represented by the membership of the South Fork Fishing and Hunting Club, asked that his name not be used, later told newspapermen:

"We were afraid of that lake . . . No one could see the immense height to which that artificial dam had been built without fearing the tremendous power of the water behind it. The dam must have had a sheer height of 100 feet, thus forcing the water that high above its natural bed and making the lake at least three miles long, out of what could scarcely be called a pond. I doubt if there is a man or woman in Johnstown who at some time or other had not feared and spoken of the terrible disaster that might ensue.

"People wondered and asked why the dam was not strengthened, as it certainly had become weak; but nothing was done, and by and by they talked less and less about it,

Johnstown

as nothing happened, though now and then some would shake their heads as if the fearful day would come sometime when their worst fears would be transcended by the horror of the actual occurrence."

Certainly there was no single Cassandra who made his or her voice ring out clearly and convincingly. A search of all the available records and newspaper files fails to turn up any person or organization deserving credit for such a warning. The prophets of disaster all sprang up on or after June 1, 1889, when they were much too late . . .

All around the ten boroughs of Johnstown the signs of a heavy flooding multiplied by the time people were up and doing that morning of May 31. At 5 A.M. there had been a landslide behind Lambert & Kress' brewery on Upper Portage street in the borough of Conemaugh. By 7 A.M. Main street was under water from Walnut street to The Point, where the rivers met just above the Stone Bridge.

The morning whistle summoned Johnstown's thousands of mill and factory workers as usual, but most of them were soon sent home. The floodwater seeping into the factories was soon swirling around the machinery. The Cambria Iron plants closed down at 7 A.M. and the Gautier wireworks sent its employes home at 10 A.M. The men went home to help their wives take up the carpets and move furniture from the first to the second floors.

The rising waters also interrupted a funeral. Mrs. Mary McNally died the previous day at her home in Prospect. Her body was removed to St. John's Roman Catholic Church at Jackson and Locust streets at 8 A.M. for the requiem mass. During the funeral services, the water rose so swiftly in the streets outside that the mourners were forced to disperse to their homes and it was impossible to proceed with the burial at the Lower Yoder cemetery. There was nothing to do but leave the casket by the altar.

In the general offices of Cambria Iron, Powell Stackhouse, the vice-president in charge of manufacturing operations—Morrell having died several years before—had just dismissed his various works managers and was conferring with Cyrus Elder, the company's general counsel.

Elder, who had just returned to Johnstown from a business trip to New York, was brought up to date on company affairs by Stackhouse, as Elder recalled in a subsequent interview with the New York *Sun*. Stackhouse told him the lower works were flooded by the time the six o'clock whistle blew and an hour later the water was running a foot deep in the other plants. The company had also received a report from the Pennsylvania Railroad's local offices that the South Fork dam had been leaking rather badly the last few days.

Elder was concerned by a more personal matter at the moment. His wife and daughter were home alone. Their home was not situated as high above the river flats as those of most of the company's top officials. Elder comforted himself with the thought that there would be some sort of warning if the flood conditions grew critical, and sufficient time for the people to evacuate the town. Telegraphic communications along the railroad from South Fork to Mineral Point to East Conemaugh to Johnstown could speed along such a warning in a matter of seconds. Both the railroad telegraph tower and the Western Union offices in Johnstown were connected by telephone with Cambria Iron's general offices. Moments after the warning was passed along, the whistles at all the plants would be tied down to sound the general alarm. Maintenance crews were assigned at all the works to keep the steam up and fires burning under the furnaces, which could be allowed to cool only at great expense.

From his window Stackhouse could survey the $50,000,-000 iron and steel empire which Daniel J. Morrell had built up over a quarter of a century of unremitting effort. Morrell had watched it grow from a scattering of blast furnaces, coke ovens and iron and coal mines to the complex industrial structure which employed from 4,000 to 6,000 workmen, depending on the volume of orders. It was ridiculous to imagine that this technological miracle could be overwhelmed by anything so elemental as the waters of Conemaugh Lake. Nature had been tamed by man and his industrial genius. The state's best engineers had constructed that dam, and it was something like treachery to the spirit of the age to doubt its worth and stability.

Yet there was an unscientific element of chance in the expansion of Cambria Iron. The company happened to be well established, thanks in large part to Morrell's vision, when the post-Civil War boom came along. A simple set of statistics indicated the reasons for that sudden flush of prosperity in the steel industry even after the orders from the War Department dwindled away. In 1864, there were 33,908 miles of railroad in the United States; ten years later there were 72,741 miles. Most of the rails had been imported for the English steelmakers at $170 a ton. Congress placed a $28-a-ton tariff on steel rails, which priced them out of the market. By 1871 Cambria Iron was able to produce steel rails at $104 a ton. The railroads which pushed across the great plains and mountains from the Mississippi to the Pacific ran, to a considerable extent, on rails produced in Johnstown.

Over in the borough of Millville towered the 75-foot

stacks of blast furnaces Nos. 1, 2, 3 and 4. Forty boilers which generated their steam were fired by furnace gas. Furnaces Nos. 5 and 6 formed a second plant, with six blowing engines supplied with steam from 32 cylindrical boilers. Near by was the Bessemer plant with its six cupolas and a battery of 21 tubular boilers supplying the steam. Nine hundred tons of ingots could be turned out by the Bessemer plant daily. In the adjacent open-hearth building, with its spectacular ten-ton traveling crane, 1,000 kegs of finished track bolts, each weighing 200 pounds, were produced monthly. The axle and forging shops near by turned out 100 finished steel axles every day.

The Gautier wireworks were now a subsidiary of Cambria Iron, the latter having bought out J. H. Gautier & Sons Company. It was housed in a large brick building, 500 by 200 feet, with a cluster of warehouses, shops and offices surrounding it. The famous Cambria Link barbed wire was manufactured here, and played almost as great a part in the conquest of western spaces as Cambria's steel rails. The barbed wire spelled the end of the open range and the great cattle baronies. The Gautier works also turned out springs, plowshares, rakes and harrows. It produced more than 50,000 tons of steel products annually, with its markets mainly in the western states.

Cambria Iron kept a firm grip on the economy of Johnstown. It maintained 35 miles of narrow-gauge railroad track, 24 locomotives and 1,500 cars to tap the surrounding hills for iron, coal and limestone; 54,423 acres of mineral land, 600 beehive coke ovens in the Connellsville district, and coal mines producing 815,000 tons a year. Cambria Iron also owned 700 dwelling places in the various boroughs. Most of them were two-family tenements without cellars, costing about $500 to build, and rented for $5 to $15 a month. They were built mostly of pine wood. When a fire broke out, it usually consumed a whole blocklong row of tenements. Cambria Iron owned all the land along the river flats, and unattractive though the flats may have been, it was the company's policy never to sell any of its real estate holdings, but only to lease. Bachelor employes were housed in a brick lodginghouse, much in the paternal British tradition of having workers "live in" and of keeping a close watch on their habits, pleasures and pastimes.

The company's paternalistic attitude was thoroughgoing, no matter what else could be said about it. It founded a woolen mill in which the widows and daughters of its workingmen could be employed. Somewhat more benevolently, it built the city's free library, donated 7,000 volumes and gave it to the city. The opera house was also built by Cambria Iron. The Cambria Mutual Benefit Association provided death, sickness and injury benefits for the employes and controlled the Cambria Hospital, which was erected just after the Civil War on Prospect Hill. For the higher echelons, the Cambria Club, housed in a pressed-brick building at Main and Federal streets, was maintained and used exclusively for the entertainment of company executives and their guests. It was before the day of the country club, and men of responsibility and dignity could not be expected to forgather in the iron-puddlers' saloons. On Washington street stood the company store, Wood, Morrell & Company, a four-story brick building crammed with all sorts of supplies for the households of Cambria Iron employes—groceries, meats, clothing, furniture, hardware, leather goods, flour and feed, salt, tobacco, shoe findings and paper hangings. The prices here were low, and gave few people cause to complain about the company's policy of keeping a hand in every human activity that stirred within the community.

Railroading was also an integral part of Johnstown's workaday life, largely because of the stream of iron and steel products that flowed out of the city. The tonnage leaving Johnstown was greater than that from most cities of 100,000 population, but the passenger traffic was so negligible that some of the Philadelphia-Pittsburgh expresses didn't even make a flag stop.

The Baltimore & Ohio ran a branch up from Rockwood, on the main line 45 miles away, but because its tracks came up from the south along the line of the less-flooded Stonycreek the B. & O.'s problems were considerably less alarming that morning than the Pennsylvania's, whose rails followed the Little Conemaugh in a generally east-west direction. Johnstown was a division point on the Pennsylvania, with a vast spread of marshaling yards, a 16-stall roundhouse and a considerable concentration of equipment in East Conemaugh.

Early that morning, around seven o'clock, Assistant Superintendent Tromp heard the reports of various subordinates, studied the telegraphic advices from Altoona and Pittsburgh, and realized that the Mountain Division was in for a spell of serious trouble. There was a landslide blocking the tracks near the summit at Lilly. Sections of track kept washing out under the heavy and continuing rainfall and the overflow of the rivers. Over on the eastern watershed of the Alleghenies the Susquehanna and the Juniata were charging over their banks and creating even more breakdowns than on the western slope of the mountains. Tromp ordered a coach coupled onto an engine and went up the line to see what could be done about getting a work train moving up to Lilly and clearing the tracks.

Meanwhile, two of the railroad's crack trains were approaching the city. The Chicago-New York Limited, eastbound, left Pittsburgh on schedule at 7:15 A.M., and the two sections of the Day Express bound for Philadelphia pulled out at 8:10 A.M. The Limited got as far as South Fork, where it was ordered to lay over until the obstruction near the town of Lilly was cleared.

The Day Express was halted a short time later in the East Conemaugh yards. All along the 40-mile stretch of track running east on the banks of the Conemaugh, the Day Express' passengers viewed an ominous spectacle from their coach and Pullman windows. The river was a boiling brownish-yellow, frothing and churning, often tearing out sections of the embankment and lashing at the tracks over which they were traveling. Saw-logs and driftwood bounded along on the crest of the flood. Occasionally drowned livestock from the hill farms up ahead bobbed in the current. There was no comfort in the arrival at Johnstown, with its streets flooded and people taking to rowboats. It had every appearance of a city slowly drowning, and the passengers hoped they wouldn't be stalled too long in such depressing surroundings.

The two sections of the Day Express were brought to a halt on separate tracks in the East Conemaugh yards, with a freight train between them. A mail train pulled up at the rear of the first section, which was composed of five day coaches, a Pullman and a baggage car. Other freights halted on adjoining tracks, waiting for a clearance to proceed.

The passengers passed through the hours in a growing despondency.

They lounged in the vestibule of the Pullman on the first

section of the Day Express, peering out the windows, watching the downpour lashing Johnstown, listening to the moaning wind. The only scenery visible was the wooded hump of a hill which rose behind the yards. On the other side was the Little Conemaugh, whose waters were rapidly encroaching on the yards.

They had only rumors to entertain them. As time passed, they grew too nervous and apprehensive to give their attention to cards, reading or casual conversation. They knew the railroad was in constant communication with its telegraph tower up at South Fork, and even those passengers unacquainted with Johnstown or the huge dam lying above the city were soon aware that there was another menace beside the rising swirl of floodwater. Members of the train crew admitted that there was reason for concern over the South Fork dam, and the passengers could see for themselves that if the reservoir was thrown into the already deluged valley their position would be hopeless. Whispers of the dam's deteriorating condition, it was later recalled, "blanched the faces of the stoutest."

By noon the rowboat and the raft had replaced the wagon and the buggy as a means of getting around downtown Johnstown. The dangers of trusting the supposed instinct of a horse to beware of dangerous footing had been demonstrated a short time earlier. At Main and Market a man driving a horse and wagon had plunged into an excavation covered with water, and the man was drowned . . . A reporter observed a number of " 'Venetians' who visited neighbors in crudely constructed craft.". . . Some of the younger blades of the city rode around the half-drowned city on horseback, showing off for the girls . . . One citizen, already marooned on the second floor of his house, was observed in a sporting mood. He was shooting rats scrambling for a refuge from the floodwaters.

At the Johnstown *Tribune* the flat-bed presses, with their banks of gas jets drying each page as it came off the forms damp with printer's ink, clanked away and produced the May 31 edition of the newspaper. It was a futile performance, for the papers wouldn't be delivered that day and the rising waters threatened to wash away the lower parts of the building where the papers were being stacked. But the newspaper business, like the theater, feels professionally bound to go through its prescribed motions, and a deadline will be regarded as sacred until the last split-second of Creation.

Upstairs in the editorial department, Editor Swank was brooding over a memorandum from his city editor, which read, "At 8:15 the Central Telephone office called the *Tribune* up to say it had been informed by Agent Deckert of the Pennsylvania Railroad freight station, that the South Fork reservoir was getting worse all the time and that the danger of its breaking was increasing momentarily." Hours before, Swank had decided to keep his staff on the job, rather than sending the reporters and printers home as most business firms in the city had done. They could work on the *Weekly Tribune,* which was circulated primarily for the farmers and residents of outlying communities, and gather a thorough report on flood damage for the next day's paper.

Out in the local room, at a desk separate from the long table at which the reporters wrote, George C. Gibbs, the assistant editor, was writing a running account of how the valley of the Little Conemaugh was enduring its annual ordeal —worse then usual this year. It was to be a sort of flood journal, to run alongside a general story which would be given the top head on Page One tomorrow, or whenever the *Tribune* next came out. Gibbs sent his story out to the composing room sheet by sheet, to be set in type immediately. Gibbs' account began:

> As we write at noon, Johnstown is again under water and all about us the tide is rising. Wagons have for hours been passing along the streets, carrying people from submerged points to places of safety, and boats, floating as jauntily as upon the bosom of a river, have traversed the thoroughfares in the lower part of town, removing pent-up inmates from homes to which partial ruin has come thrice within as many years. We hear of lives sacrificed, the Rolling Mill shut down, costly bridges swept away, great landslides which block the railroads, penning in trains where they were forced to stop upon the track, log booms bursted, cellars filled the whole town over, the streets as far up and back as Jackson running with the yellow, devastating flood. A most exasperating state of affairs, and one for which there ought to be a remedy.
>
> So the hours wore on, full only of excitement for some, but of hard, fatiguing work and increasing distress for many others. Now would run over the town a rumor of a man drowned, of horses perishing, of daring rescuers or dashing adventurers nearly losing their lives, and the hello bell in the Central [Telephone] Office was hot with the impatient jingle of repeated calls. Johnstown, Cambria, the upper boroughs—wherever the telephone line ends—at the end of each wire was a worried listener or a man or woman excitedly asking someone else how it fared with them. What a blessing the telephone was, and how, if it could feel, it must have tingled with modest thoughts of its great usefulness . . .

The perfect prototype for a Horatio Alger widow was Mrs. Harriet M. Ogle, manager of the Johnstown office of Western Union. Her husband had been killed in action during the Civil War and she was left with three children to support. It was hard enough for a woman to earn her own living in those days as a seamstress or in some other exclusively feminine occupation. Mrs. Ogle invaded a field as sternly masculine as chewing tobacco and mustache cups.

Telegraphy was a craft in those days for men who didn't want to settle down. Most operators were freelance types who liked to wander from town to town, working in commercial telegraph offices, railroad towers or newspaper offices. The footloose "puncher" was a picturesque addition to the floating population, the boomers and drifters, like tramp reporters, itinerant printers, tinkers, bindle stiffs, harvest hands, prospectors—the whole backwash of the now vanished frontier. He was often a boozer, inclined toward a nonviolent anarchy, with no yearning for home, marriage, or lodge nights.

Mrs. Ogle had no use for this carefree way of life. She "didn't hold" with boozing, tobacco-chewing or loose language. She had a stern sense of duty, and not a little of the top sergeant in her character. Western Union had first hired her, against its better judgment, as its sole representative in Johnstown. She was given an assistant, later a number of employes as the city and its commercial telegraph traffic grew. Her superiors in the Pittsburgh office considered her one of their best branch managers. Since she always signed her reports "H. M. Ogle" in a round masculine hand, most of the higher echelons in Western Union believed the Johnstown manager was a man, and Pittsburgh did not disillusion them.

Mrs. Ogle, plump, bustling and in her mid-forties, was calm and self-possessed as the waters rose in the streets outside her office. At 1 A.M. she gave orders to abandon the first floor and move up to the third. That meant they were cut off from the central telephone office, whose booth was on the first floor. A number of people were lined up at the telephone booth, trying to reach their homes or neighbors who were on the telephone circuit. (There were several hundred phones in Johnstown, most of them in commercial use.)

Mrs. Ogle and her daughter Minnie, who was her chief assistant, moved upstairs with the four operators and three messengers who comprised the Johnstown office of Western Union. There were few commercial messages to be passed along that day, but Mrs. Ogle saw to it that towns up and down the valley received all the latest news of the flood situation.

"No one," she announced firmly, "is to leave the office. We may be needed, and we must stay at our posts."

Shortly after 3 P.M. she relayed her last message. It was to Charles O. Rowe, manager of the Pittsburgh office.

"SOUTH FORK OPERATOR SAYS THE DAM IS ABOUT TO GO,"

it read.

Along toward two o'clock Cyrus Elder, general counsel for Cambria Iron, found himself worrying about his wife and daughter at home. There would be little he could do for them if the South Fork dam burst, which he still refused to believe would happen, but he'd feel better himself if he were with them. Elder was not exactly the typical company lawyer. In the first place, he had a sense of humor—not always prominent in the legal profession—and secondly, and secretly, he wrote poetry. (His secret was revealed in 1909 when *Poems*, by Cyrus Elder, was published by J. B. Lippincott Company.) Elder set out with two employes in a skiff. They were paddling through the downtown section when the boat was upset by a strong current coming up from the

Little Conemaugh opposite Griffiths' drugstore in the park. "Mr. Elder did not tumble out," wrote a reporter for the *Tribune* who observed the incident from the window of his second-story office, "but with great presence of mind stood up in the torrent and took his little wetting, afterward walking off in the water and leaving the boat behind." The Reverend H. L. Chapman later recalled in his *Memoirs of an Itinerant* (privately published, undated) that the dunking did not deprive Elder of his sense of humor. The lawyer called to Reverend Chapman, in another boat, "Have you got any fishing tackle, Reverend? I might as well make use of my time here." Elder was rescued by a man with a high-wheeled wagon, but it was impossible to proceed farther along Walnut street, where his home was located. He went to his brother's home on higher ground, praying that Mrs. Elder and their 23-year-old daughter Nannie would be safe in their stoutly built brick house.

Frederick Krebs, a works superintendent at the Gautier division of Cambria Iron, knew it would be a bad day when he took the trolley to work that morning and the passengers had to get out and walk because a landslide blocked the tracks. He found the workers in the rolling mill standing around, up to their shoe-tops in floodwater. Some of them reminded him that the borough of Conemaugh, right where they stood, had been under five or six feet of water some years before the Gautier works were built.

"All right," Krebs said with a shrug. "Close down after you roll out whatever steel is left in the heating furnace, and go home to your families. No doubt your wives will have more work for you than you'll find around here today."

Shortly before noon Krebs rolled down the top of his desk and walked home for dinner—not for many years would the meal be called lunch. At his home on Napoleon street, which was running a foot of water from the Stonycreek near by, he found that Mrs. Krebs had a guest for dinner, her cousin, Dr. Harriet Jones, a physician from Terra Alta, West Virginia. As they sat down and Krebs saw that they had an unusually elaborate midday meal in honor of Dr. Jones, he ventured on a pleasantry:

"Enjoy this meal, it may be a long time before we sit down to such a dinner."

Alexander Adair and Richard Eyre were trudging up the railroad tracks from Cambria City, where they owned property and had been inspecting some houses, to Johnstown. The bridge at Cambria City had been knocked out and there was no other way of returning to the city. A westbound freight approached, and the engineer slowed down long enough to shout, "They've just got a warning in East Conemaugh that the South Fork dam might break any minute. Pass the word along and fly to the hills!"

For years a sure-fire laugh was to be raised by shouting, "The dam has busted—run for the hills." The engineer, his face white with fear, obviously wasn't trying to get a laugh. Adair and Eyre agreed they had better retrace their footsteps and spread the alarm. They soon found it was the old story of "crying wolf." People to whom they shouted the warning only shook their heads, laughed and said, "We've heard that one before." They came across the burgess of Cambria City, Edward E. O'Neill, and told him of the report received by the railroad at its East Conemaugh yards. He shrugged and said, "I'll pass the news along, but I won't expect the people to pay much attention. It's an old story with them."

Feeling more than a little frustrated, Adair and Eyre

walked back up the tracks to Johnstown. They were beginning to wonder if they hadn't been taken in by that engineer.
Crossing the Stone Bridge, they noticed that the water
seemed to be falling slightly; the crest had been reached
and passed safely, and by tomorrow morning, if the South
Fork dam held, the only damage would be a few bridges
wrecked and mud deposited liberally over the city. But
they met Squire William C. Bland, of Millville, and he had
heard the same report from East Conemaugh.

The time was 3:15 P.M.

They had done all they could to warn their fellow citizens.

Adair and Eyre decided to take that engineer's advice and
"fly to the hills."

Several hundred persons in the course of the day were
sufficiently alarmed to take to the high ground which, fortunately, rose all around the city. One family which took
alarm by noontime was that of A. Dix Tittle Sr. Tittle was
a widower living on Locust street with his two motherless
sons and two daughters. During the morning Tittle heard
that some of the bridges were under water and that the
steel companies had run trains out on them to hold them
in place. Actually this was an unfounded rumor, but it
served to persuade Tittle to take his family to a safer place.

His son Dix Jr. recalled in later years how he and his
brother and sisters huddled under a tree against the pouring
rain and stared down the hillside as the rising rivers blotted
out street after street. A number of other families grouped
themselves, somewhat shamefacedly, under other trees
along the brow of the hill. Dix Jr. and most of the boys
among those who had taken refuge on the hill felt a little foolish and unheroic. They could imagine what their

friends would say when the water receded and they trooped back to their homes. "Fraidy cat, fraidy cat" would probably be the mildest epithet. Most of their friends down below were wading around the streets in rubber boots and having a wonderful time. The boys on the hilltop could only wish their fathers had allowed them to stay down where all the fun was.

Some of the solider buildings in Johnstown were the hotels grouped around the intersection of Clinton and Main streets. The intersection was almost a mile above The Point, where the Little Conemaugh and the Stonycreek met, and the water was much lower in the upper end of Main street. The Keystone was the smallest but not, it developed, the frailest. The Merchants was an old-fashioned three-story tavern. The Fritz Hotel was an ornately furnished, narrow, four-story brick building.

But the pride of Johnstown was the new Hulbert House, four stories high and topped with an elegant mansard roof. This, it was generally agreed, was the safest place in town at a time of high water.

J. L. Smith, a stone mason, was thinking about the Hulbert House as he worked in the marble and granite works next to his home at 202 Stonycreek street. His house was one of a row standing on the bank of the Stonycreek River. By noon the river was rampaging over its banks. Smith hurried into the house and told his wife he was taking her and their three children to the Hulbert House for a safer refuge.

Mrs. Smith protested. She wasn't "dressed properly" to associate with the prosperous travelers who stopped off at the Hulbert House on their way through Johnstown. But Smith was adamant, and took his wife and children to the hotel at Main and Clinton streets. Then he returned to his stone-cutting works to "look after my property," well content that his family was safe.

One of the solider citizens of Johnstown was W. Horace Rose, attorney-at-law and a prominent Democrat in a town where the powers-that-be were 100 percent Republican. He had served as burgess of Johnstown, as a member of the state legislature and as district attorney of Cambria county. Now 51 years old, he was a veteran of the Civil War and still carried himself like a soldier. He had gone off to war with the 54th Pennsylvania Volunteers as a private; soon commissioned, he served as an assistant adjutant general on the brigade staff, was wounded in northern Virginia and recovered in time to participate in General Sheridan's scourging of the Valley of the Shenandoah.

Rose, gray of hair and beard, with a big aggressive nose, sharp gray eyes and a determined-looking jaw, was the father of four stalwart sons and a daughter. It was just as well that the Rose boys were stalwart for they were given four rather dainty names, Horace, Percy, Winter and Forest.

That morning Rose ate a leisurely breakfast, knowing the high water would curtail all legal business, listened to the report of his 14-year-old son Percy that both rivers were rising, and ordered Percy to drive the family milk cow up the hillside so they wouldn't have to worry about her if the flooding continued. The lawyer then hitched up his buggy with the second-best harness and set out on a tour of the flooded downtown streets. At Main and Clinton, he paused to exchange greetings with an old friend, Charles Zimmerman, and watch a cow bend its neck and drink floodwater. "Charley," Rose said, "you and I have scored 50 years, and this is the first time we ever saw a cow drink Stonycreek river water on Main street." *

Rose drove over to his law office on Franklin street, only 100 feet from the Stonycreek. He recalled that the flood of '87 had left one foot of water in his office, and "immediately set about placing my papers above the flood line of '87." There was nothing to do at the office but watch the water seeping in, so he started back toward his house on upper Main street. Along the way he met one of his neighbors, John Dibert, the banker, who was also treasurer of the borough of Johnstown. The two men discussed the causes of the annual floodings and what could be done about it. Rose cited the fact that, by agreement with Cambria Iron, the channel of the Little Conemaugh had been narrowed to 110 feet, that of the Stonycreek to 175 feet. That made a total of 285 feet of waterway above the confluence of the rivers. But Cambria Iron had also narrowed the channel of the Conemaugh below the confluence to less than 200 feet. Rose and Dibert agreed that a citizens' committee should be organized as soon as possible to compel Cambria Iron to dredge the channel below where the two rivers join and "restore the stream to its original width and give an outlet for the waters."

The attorney arrived home at 11 A.M. and found that the floodwater had risen all around his house. He had to build a flimsy raft of logs on high ground near by and float himself over to the back porch of his house. He helped his wife and sons take up carpets and furniture and "marked with sadness that water was staining the beautiful paper I had recently put upon the walls of my dwelling." He took some comfort in the fact most of his family was gathered around

---

* Quoted from Rose's account of his flood experiences in the Reverend David J. Beale's *Through the Johnstown Flood,* Philadelphia, 1889.

him. Forest, his 16-year-old, had taken refuge with neighbors across the street when the water on Main street rose too high for easy wading. Winter, the 20-year-old, and Percy, the youngest, were home, and Horace, the 27-year-old eldest son had come over to help his parents. Once the furniture-moving was finished, the family gathered in an upstairs sitting room, where Mrs. Rose and her daughter built a fire of boxwood in the grate, boiled coffee over it and served it in tin cups. A morning of discomfort and inconvenience had suddenly turned into a family picnic. The senior Rose, usually a man of great dignity, was in exceptionally high spirits; he felt, he later recalled with a sense of wonder, like a schoolboy released for an unexpected holiday, and leaned out the window to joke with neighbors similarly beleaguered by the floodwaters on the second floors of their homes. As the afternoon wore on, the water seemed to be falling slightly. It never crossed his mind, he said later, that there might be trouble brewing in the hills above the city.

In a new three-story red brick house at Jackson and Main streets lived part of one of the more closely knit families in Johnstown. The sons-in-law not only married into the family but the family business, the dry-goods store of Geis, Foster & Quinn. The store was founded by John and Rosina Geis. Their daughter Rosina married James Quinn, a Civil War cavalry officer; Barbara married Andrew Foster, and both Foster and Quinn were taken into the store as partners. A third daughter was Mrs. Mary O'Brien, who lived in nearby Scottdale.

The house at Jackson and Main was the home of the Quinns, a spacious and comfortable place designed for a growing family and only a few doors away from the "dear little old-fashioned brick house painted white with green shutters" where the elderly Geises lived. The description, and the history of the Geis-Foster-Quinn family on May 31 and the days that followed, come from one of the most vivid of family chronicles, *Johnstown and Its Flood* (Wilkes-Barre, 1936), which Gertrude Quinn Slattery wrote for her own children. Gertrude then was an eight-year-old, the daughter of James Quinn. In the account written 47 years later, she recalled in remarkable detail the events of that day, recalled them as only a sensitive and intelligent child could have registered them in her mind.

It was a most comfortable and secure world, then, for a middle-class family. The profits from the dry-goods store supported all three households in the solid and substantial style valued by proper Victorians.

Gertrude always remembered her father and his brother-in-law, Andrew Foster, as resembling the Smith Brothers of cough-drop fame, because each had almost identical beards. Gertrude, her brother and three sisters were raised in an atmosphere in which slight irreverences were not frowned upon. One of the jokes she remembered from her childhood was a Sunday School teacher's question, "Johnny, who made the world?" and Johnny's quick and confident reply: "The Cambria Iron Company."

On the morning of May 31, James Quinn presided alone over the family breakfast table. He and his wife had gone over to Scottdale a few days before to stand up as godparents at the christening of the youngest child of Mrs. Quinn's sister. Rosina Quinn stayed in Scottdale for a longer visit with her sister. In her absence, the Quinn children were being cared for by their 24-year-old aunt, Mrs. Abbie Ludes, who was visiting the Quinns from her home in Salinas, Kansas, with her two-year-old son Richard, and by their nurse, Mary Libby.

Johnstown

Gertrude always remembered that morning, dark with foreboding, the air thick as "the smoke of brushwood fires." And her father, one of the few residents who seemed to be concerned over the condition of the South Fork dam, saying, "I've been worrying about that dam night and day for the past week." James Quinn went from his breakfast to the store farther down Main street to superintend the removal of the more valuable merchandise to a barn on higher ground outside the flooded downtown section. During the morning the water crept up Main street to the level of the curbstones around Jackson street, and throughout the neighborhood could be heard the voices of boys splashing around and having the time of their lives. Gertrude could only envy them. She was an unabashed tomboy, but her aunt and Nurse Libby had forbidden her to leave the yard. Her 16-year-old brother Vincent was among the rubber-booted frolickers.

By the time her father came home at noon for dinner, Gertrude noticed that the floodwater had advanced from the curb and was deep enough in the lower part of their front lawn to allow the family's ducklings to paddle around. "Yellow gurgling water" was creeping over the whole neighborhood, isolating the houses in a shallow but encroaching sea.

James Quinn, seated magisterially at the head of the dinner table, was even more concerned than he had been at breakfast, and warned the family to be prepared for a sudden move up Green Hill, which rose abruptly a hundred yards behind the Quinn house.

"If the dam gives way," Quinn told his family, "not a brick would be left standing in this town . . . I'd take you up there right now if it weren't for little Marie." Gertrude's infant sister had the measles and was lying in the darkened nursery up on the third floor.

"Oh, James, you are too anxious," Gertrude's Aunt Abbie said. "This big house would never go."

"I have seen the dam," Quinn said somewhat curtly. "It is a mighty body of water at any time, and now with the continuous rain it is a very dangerous proposition for the people of Johnstown."

Abbie Ludes turned to Nurse Libby and commented, "Mr. Quinn is too fearful." The fact that her aunt came from "dry and sunny Kansas," Gertrude believed, rendered her incapable of "imagining the flood that my father feared."

Gertrude excused herself from the table and wandered out on the porch. Her father had ordered her not to get her feet wet and risk a cold by leaving the porch, but Gertrude was fascinated by the picture of the half-drowned pansy bed out on the lawn and waded out for a closer look. "This is a picture I can't forget," she wrote later, "those little purple faces lying on the water."

Her father came out on the porch to light a cigar—one concession that well-trained husbands made to their women-folk in those days was to smoke outside the house—and noticed that his daughter had disobeyed his instructions. Gertrude gave him more trouble than all three of his other daughters. "My little white head," he called her in token of her ash-blond hair. She was a winsome child with lively blue eyes and an impish smile. Quinn could not help secretly sympathizing with her attempts to resist being cast in the conventional mold of all the other starched, dainty and curtsying little girls. There was something a little different, both prideful and pixyish, about Gertrude.

But there was also such a thing as family discipline, and James Quinn placed a considerable value on discipline. Although middle-aged, he still looked every inch the cavalry officer who rode with his regiment in the Tennessee campaigns of the Army of the Cumberland during the Civil War.

So Quinn, mindful of discipline, paddled his little daughter and sent her upstairs to put on dry shoes and stockings. He chewed on his cigar and kept looking up the valley of the Little Conemaugh. Some instinct, he later told his daughter, kept him rooted there, standing guard.

Late in the afternoon the floodwaters seemed to be receding slightly. The worst of the storm appeared to be over as four o'clock approached.

Down at the *Tribune*, George Gibbs, writing his running account of the flood, felt the situation had improved enough to inject a humorous sidelight in his story for the weekly edition: "People who were glad they didn't live downtown began to wish they didn't live in town at all . . ."

4. The Dam Breaks

THE NIGHT of May 30-31 in the countryside around Conemaugh Lake was a meteorological nightmare. There were cloudbursts in the mountains, waterspouts in the valley of South Fork Run, and the roar of floodwater from all directions. The waterspouts were particularly mischievous, tearing holes ten feet deep in the loam and clay soil around Conemaugh Lake. One witness of the damage done by the waterspouts said, "It looked as if a powerful shovel, with an area of many feet, had been dashed into the ground by some mighty force and with a twirl had torn out an immense chunk of earth."

The Heidenfelter family, which operated a tannery on the west shore of the lake, was terrified by the unusual disturbance. "We were awakened at 10:20 P.M. by the roaring," Mrs. Heidenfelter later told a reporter. "I never heard anything like it in my life. I wanted my husband to get up and see what the matter was, but it was dark and he could have done no good. In the morning as soon as we could see, the fields were covered with water four or five feet deep. People say the noise was a waterspout but I've never seen one and don't know how they act. One thing I do know, and that is I thought the day of judgment had come when the roaring and awful rain happened. It sounded just as if a big tank had opened at the bottom and all the water was falling out at once."

For all its suggestions of the supernatural to Mrs. Heidenfelter, the waterspout actually is a freakish, funnel-shaped cloud that plays over the surface or in the vicinity of a large body of water, loosing its rivetlike jets of water, somewhat like a miniature tornado. Other residents of the lake shore were frightened by it, and a farmer who had lived in the neighborhood for 37 years said it was the worst storm of his experience.

Another early riser among the lake dwellers was Colonel Unger, president of the South Fork sportsmen's club. He awakened to a sound he had been hearing at intervals all night—rain on the roof. It was still pelting down, steadily as when he had drifted uneasily into sleep. Unger clambered out of bed in his third-floor room in the clubhouse and looked out the window. The lake was obscured by a heavy fog, but he could hear the roar of water above the drumming of the rain.

Unger was keenly aware of the burden of responsibility that rested upon him that morning. It was too late to consult by telegraph or telephone with his fellow club members in Pittsburgh; yet if he ordered the gratings on the spillways removed, and possibly other emergency measures taken, he would look like a fool if the rain suddenly stopped and the threat to the dam suddenly eased. At the very least a summer's fishing would be ruined and the lake would have to be restocked.

He had been flattered by his election as president of the club, especially since he had nothing approaching the social or financial prestige of most of his fellow club members. Unger had reason to suspect that he had been handed the honor largely because his home was in the vicinity and he

The Dam Breaks

had had considerable hotel experience before retiring to his native mountains. The 59-year-old colonel, the origins of whose military rank are not explained in the *Biographical and Portrait Cyclopedia of Cambria County*, was an Eisenhower on his mother's side, a prominent and ubiquitous Pennsylvania Dutch family. His career began as a route agent, brakeman and conductor on the Pennsylvania Railroad. For many years he managed the railroad's chain of hotels stretching through its territory from Pittsburgh to Jersey City, then became the proprietor of the Seventh Avenue Hotel in Pittsburgh. When he retired in 1888, he bought a 250-acre stretch of land along Lake Conemaugh. Since he lived near by, the other members felt he could keep a close eye on the club's property, particularly if he was honored with the presidency.

Unger would have liked to crawl back under the covers until the whole infernal crisis had passed, but his sense of duty would not let him shirk. His fellow clubmen trusted him to do the right thing. Slowly and reluctantly he pulled on his clothes and went downstairs. It was a few minutes before half-past six.

John Parke, the young civil engineer, was waiting for him in the common room on the first floor. His high boots and breeches spattered with mud, Parke obviously had undertaken an inspection at first light.

"How bad?" Unger asked curtly.

"The water at the dam has risen two feet during the night," Parke reported. "Around the shores of the lake it's rising at the rate of three feet an hour. I'd say the feeders were pouring 3,000,000 gallons an hour into the lake. If that keeps up all morning—"

"No sign of a letup in the rain?"

"I'm no weather prophet, sir, but looks like an all-day

storm to me. The water in the spillway is running seven and a half feet high, and the gratings are clogged with branches and all sorts of debris brought down from the mountains."

Unger shook himself, breathed deep, and said, "Then the gratings will have to come out. There's no other choice. Let's get the workmen busy on that right away."

"They're having breakfast right now, and I'd like to take a look at the upper end of the lake."

Unger suggested that Parke row up to the head of the lake to take a look at the feeders while he took charge of the workmen at the dam. Parke agreed. He set out in the rowboat immediately, having noted that the lake had risen five inches in the short time he spent waiting for and talking to Colonel Unger. The feeders, he found, were roaring like millraces, draining a 52-square-mile watershed.

The engineer rowed back to the landing at the clubhouse and joined Colonel Unger at the dam.

By that time it was evident that Colonel Unger's agonizing decision to lift the fish gratings on the spillway was of no avail. The workmen were unable to budge the heavy iron grids, tangled as they were with branches and other debris. Unger and Parke looked at each other in dismay. Both had counted on opening the spillway to relieve considerable pressure from the overburdened dam.

"What can we do now, Parke?" Unger asked, his voice edged with despair. "Could we try cutting another spillway through the western end of the dam?"

The rush of water trying to burst through the dam was too clamorous to allow a discussion on the spot. Parke drew Unger away from the dam so they could make themselves heard without shouting and without being overheard by the workmen.

"It's probably too late to dig another spillway," Parke told

Unger, "but we have the men and the shovels, and anything's worth a try under the circumstances. It's almost solid rock at the other end and the men won't be able to dig very deep in the next few hours. Not deep enough to take a great amount of pressure off the dam. The water's less than six feet from the crest of the dam right now. When it reaches the top and starts flowing over it, the dam's through."

"There's always a chance those feeders will stop pouring into the lake."

"Yes, there's a chance. . . ."

By noon it was obvious that cutting a new channel around the western end of the dam would divert only a trickle of water. The trench dug by the workmen, flailing away at the rocky terrain with their picks, knowing that the fate of the town below depended to a great extent on their efforts, was pathetically inadequate. It was only two feet wide and 14 inches deep.

The level of the lake had reached the crest of the dam at 11:30 A.M.

From now on, Parke knew, it was touch and go.

Shortly after eleven o'clock Herbert Webber, the club's handyman, caretaker and guardian of the hunting preserves, noticed that the level of the lake seemed to be lowering. He had been working on the grounds of a cottage a mile up the lake shore from the dam. Wondering if the dam had given way, he ran down to the lower end of the reservoir. The dam was still in business, but it was leaking worse than ever. One jet of water shot out 30 feet from the dam and leaped into the valley below, and Webber could see water welling through the foundation stones of the dam.

Webber stayed at the dam site; he had plenty of work to do, getting the cottages ready for the first members on the summer list, scheduled for the latter part of June, but there was a dread fascination about watching a man's fearful prophecies come true . . . especially when they had been so rudely rejected.

Other men were watching the dam, too, among them Dan Sibert, an employe of the Argyle Coal Company, who had been stationed there by J. P. Wilson, superintendent of the mining company. Sibert kept riding back and forth between the dam and the village of South Fork to keep Wilson informed of the situation. When Wilson learned that great jets of water were spouting from the dam, he went to the South Fork telegraph tower of the Pennsylvania Railroad and demanded that the operator on duty, Miss Emma Ehrenfield, send a warning message down the valley:

THE DAM IS GETTING WORSE AND MAY POSSIBLY GO.

Miss Ehrenfield was reluctant to send such an alarmist message but Wilson said he would take the responsibility and sign the warning himself.

The next tower down the line was a mile west of Mineral Point. William H. Pickerill, the operator, was far more impressed by the warning than Miss Ehrenfield. He sent word to his family, including his wife and four children, to evacuate their home in the village of Mineral Point and wait up on the mountainside until he let them know the danger was past. Pickerill was a sensible and cautious man. No boomer like many of his fellow operators, he had studied for his trade at the Commercial Business and Telegraph College in Oberlin, Ohio, and took his work seriously. A man in a railroad telegraph tower was responsible for many lives. Then 37 years old, he had never been given an official demerit for the slightest infraction of the company's rules. Other people might take the flood situation lightly but he was a family man and knew the tragedies that might result from anyone in a responsible position laughing off such warnings. He kept relaying hourly reports to the main tower down in East Conemaugh.

Up at the dam John Parke decided the situation was hopeless. The dam would break in a matter of hours. There was nothing left to do but spread the alarm, get the warning to Johnstown in time for people to reach the hilltops all around them. The engineer mounted his horse and rode at a gallop north toward the village of South Fork, which was almost two miles away. He stopped at the Fisher and Lamb farms along the way to warn those families that the dam couldn't last much longer and they must move to the rim of the valley. He also alerted everyone he saw on the streets of South Fork, crying, "The dam can't last more than a few hours. Get to higher ground as fast as you can!" Not everyone took him seriously.

A few minutes later he strode into the South Fork tower of the railroad and, white-faced and tense with excitement, paused only to tell Miss Ehrenfield: "Warn Johnstown that the dam is about to break!"

Before Miss Ehrenfield could speak, however, Parke turned and hurried out of the tower, mounting his horse and heading back to the dam. What the woman operator started to tell him was that the lines to Johnstown were now inoperative. The telegraph poles had been washed out along the flooded tracks west of Mineral Point. Still she could, and did, relay the warning down to the Mineral Point tower. It was one of many warnings sent down the line that day; it should have been the most impressive, but Parke was youthful, a stranger in the locality, and no special emphasis was given his bulletin.

Parke rode back to the dam believing, as he said later, that "everybody in the Conemaugh region did or should have known of the danger," and it wasn't until several days later that he learned his message never reached Johnstown. There was nothing left to do at the dam. The erosive power of the sheet of water behind it could not be withstood; the center of the dam was a mere fretwork of mud, sticks and stones, and crevices the size of barrels had opened up in the face of the structure.

Shortly after 3 P.M. a V-shaped notch ten feet deep was suddenly gouged out of the center.

A few minutes later the whole propulsive energy of twenty million tons of water was directed at the weak spot.

At 3:10 P.M. the center of the dam gave way with a "thunderous report" that echoed against the walls of the valley. Lake Conemaugh leaped from its artificial bed at the bottom of the ravine and plunged down the South Fork valley. Ahead of it, like a boy aimlessly kicking a football along, the flood tide pushed the fragments of a 300-foot-long segment of the dam.

"The dam did not burst," Parke reported later. "It simply moved away. The water gradually ate into the embankment until there was nothing left but a frail bulwark of wood. This finally split asunder and sent the waters howling down the mountains."

Parke, the workmen, Colonel Unger, other employes of the club and several residents of the vicinity could only stand and watch the lake empty itself of water, flood debris from the mountains, the docks, the fleet of pleasure craft. It was an awesome spectacle. Crouse, the manager of the clubhouse, said that "when the dam broke the water seemed to leap, scarcely touching the ground. It bounded down the valley, crashing and roaring, carrying everything before it."

Herbert Webber watched the lake drain itself away in

The Dam Breaks

less than an hour, and said that by four o'clock, 50 minutes after the dam collapsed, the level of the lake was so low it "showed bottom 50 feet below" the former shoreline on which he stood.

Another eyewitness was the Reverend G. W. Brown, pastor of the South Fork United Brethren Church. "Having heard the rumor that the reservoir was leaking, I went up to see for myself. It was ten minutes of three. When I approached, the water was running over the breast of the dam to the depth of about a foot. The first break in the earthen surface, made a few minutes later, was large enough to admit the passage of a train of cars. When I witnessed this, I exclaimed, 'God have mercy on the people below'. . .

"The dam melted away . . . Only a few minutes were required to make an opening more than 300 feet wide and down to the bottom. I watched it until the wall that held back the waters was torn away, and the entire lake began to move and finally, with a tremendous rush that made the hills quake, the vast body of water was poured out into the valley below. Only about 45 minutes were required to precipitate those millions of tons of water upon the unsuspecting inhabitants of the Conemaugh valley. Onward dashed the flood, roaring like a mighty battle, tree-top high, toward South Fork village, rolling over and over again rocks that weighed tons and tons, carrying them a mile or more from the spot where they had lain for ages."

Two farm families, the Fishers and the Lambs, who lived in the South Fork valley below the dam, barely escaped with their lives—and nothing else. George Fisher had hauled his milk wagon, plow and other equipment to higher ground, but it wasn't high enough and the first wave of the flood snatched them away like toys. His neighbor, George Lamb, almost sacrificed himself and his family for the sake of their

81

two pigs, according to a New York *Sun* reporter, who wrote that Lamb stayed in his house "until he heard the thunder of the waters pouring through the first breach in the dam. Then he shouted to neighbors who had come running down the hill to rescue his wife and children, while he ran himself to save the pigs. He didn't get the pigs. If the neighbors hadn't helped him out along with his family he would have been caught in the first rush of the torrent. He got back to high ground in time to see his house climb the face of the great wall of water. He saw it roll and toss for an instant with Fisher's house, and then they were both flung against the bluff with a force that dashed them into splinters. Not a fragment of them was found after the water had subsided."

Down at South Fork, the railroad telegraph tower had dispatched its last message an hour before, reading:

THE WATER IS RUNNING OVER THE BREAST OF THE LAKE. DAM IN CENTRE AND WEST SIDE IS BECOMING DANGEROUS.

Then the line went dead.

William Pickerill, the operator at Mineral Point, received the message and forwarded it to the main tower at East Conemaugh. He knew it was received because his instrument clicked out the call letters "J.O.," which were those of Montgomery, the operator at East Conemaugh. These and previous warnings were passed along to the Central Telephone Company, which in turn called its subscribers. But few persons acted on them. In the boroughs below, as the *Sun* reporter wrote, "The previous cries of 'Wolf!' made the cry ineffective now that the wolf was at the doorstep. Only the timid and the prudent escaped the coming flood by going to the hillsides in time. For the others, the only notice was the ringing of the bell at the Cambria Iron works, but so brief was this notice that the bell had not stopped ringing

The Dam Breaks

when the flood came. There was no time for even the bell-ringer to escape."

Once the reservoir broke loose from the dam, it hurtled down South Fork Run to its mouth two miles away. The flood front had a crest 40 feet high. To point up the force and violence of that juggernaut, John B. McMaster, an engineering professor who made a painstaking study of the flood (the manuscript of which has been deposited with the Historical Society of Pennsylvania), wrote that "it would have made a stream 500 feet wide, 20 feet deep and 12 miles long. It would have taken 36 minutes to go over Niagara Falls at the same depth and velocity of the Niagara River." When it reached the confluence of the Little Conemaugh, the amount of water in that already flooded channel was doubled.

The flood crashed against the mountain on the north bank of the Little Conemaugh and washed upstream far enough to tear out an iron bridge. It swept over the evacuated village of South Fork. Then it started down the Little Conemaugh on its 14-mile sweep through a heavy industrialized valley to Johnstown.

The Chicago-New York Limited, eastbound, had been waiting on the tracks just west of South Fork for five hours while railroad crews labored up the line to clear away a landslide between South Fork and Kittaning. The engineer caught sight of the flood wave bearing down on the village and immediately started the train racing across the bridge over the Little Conemaugh only a few seconds before the flood wave reached it. The water from the dam struck the bridge, tossed it into the air and carried it downstream. A freight train stacked up behind the Chicago-New York Limited was less fortunate. The flood toppled its pusher engine and carried the boxcars downstream.

Johnstown

In the telegraph tower west of Mineral Point, Operator Pickerill, his lines dead in both directions, had no warning of the disaster except the roar of the floodwater, followed a few moments later by the spectacle of human beings bobbing downstream on its crest. A few hundred feet west of the tower an engine waited on the tracks. Pickerill shouted down to the engineer John Hess, "The dam's broken—clear out or you'll be washed off the tracks!" Hess tied down his whistle and raced his engine backwards toward East Conemaugh. The shrieking train whistle was the only real warning received by that borough. Hess didn't stop until he reached the east end of the yards; then he jumped out of the engine and ran up Railroad street to his home, arriving in time to gather up his family and take them to the safety of a hillside. The train whistle blasted away behind him. It didn't stop until the flood picked up the engine, choked its boiler and swept it downstream.

The village of Mineral Point was completely destroyed by the flood, all 32 of its houses and the woodworking plant of the Cambria Iron Company torn from their foundations. Sixteen persons lost their lives. The telegraph tower was toppled, too, but not before Operator Pickerill fled to higher ground a few yards away. The stone viaduct which carried the tracks of the Pennsylvania Railroad across the Little Conemaugh, 70 feet above the normal level of the river, was snapped "like a pipe of clay" and dashed to pieces.

The great wall of water, rolling, lashing and writhing in a monstrous frenzy, bore down on the "twin boroughs" of East Conemaugh, on the north bank of the Little Conemaugh, and Franklin, on the south bank just opposite, six miles west of Mineral Point. The Reverend J. A. Smith of the Franklin United Brethren Church heard Engineer Hess' whistle shrieking and looked out an upstairs window of his home in Franklin. He saw the engine stop "just opposite the house of Master Mechanic Spane" across the river and "here Hess abandoned his engine, still sounding out the alarm, while he ran to his home near by and carried his family to the hills just in the nick of time." A moment later Reverend Smith caught sight of the towering flood wave. The minister's house stood high enough to survive. All he could do was to fall on his knees and begin praying.

In the East Conemaugh yards the Day Express, eastbound, was still laying over, waiting for word that the tracks near the summit had been cleared. The water kept rising on the tracks, and few of the passengers could conceal their apprehension; still, they depended on the railroad to get them out of there if the situation grew really dangerous. It was clearly the railroad's responsibility to remove them to a point of safety. The Pennsylvania always knew what it was doing; hadn't it risen to the Civil War and other emergencies with the greatest efficiency? Yet many of the passengers couldn't help feeling that the Day Express had been shunted into the yards and forgotten. Perhaps the railroad had more to worry about than 50-odd passengers and their baggage.

In the first section, 20-year-old Jennie Paulson, a slender and vivacious girl from Allegheny City, and her traveling companion, Elizabeth Bryan, also 20, of Philadelphia, were chattering unconcernedly. They and the children on the train were the only ones who refused to worry. At least one of the other passengers bitterly envied them their youthful unconcern. All that bothered Jennie Paulson at the moment was the fact that she was invited to attend a week-end house party at Miss Bryan's home in Philadelphia. She hoped she would be equal to the social demands of the occasion.

Johnstown

Near by in their Pullman seats sat Charles A. Richwood and his bride, Edith. They had been married the previous afternoon in Pittsburgh, had endured a cramped and distressing night in transit, and were on their way to New York. They had counted on finding themselves amid the solid comforts of the Fifth Avenue Hotel by nightfall, but now they had spent hour after hour on this miserable siding and knew they would not reach New York until the early hours of the next morning.

It was getting along toward four o'clock, the rain kept pelting down, the river kept slowly rising.

Far up the valley was heard the approaching shriek of Engineer Hess' whistle. People craned their necks to look up the tracks, conscious of the urgency implied in the continued whistling. Conductor Bell hurried to the platform outside the Pullman, conferred hastily with the Pullman porter, Frank Phillips, and the two brakemen on the train. They agreed the whistle must be a signal that something serious had happened upriver. The trainmen split up and hurried through the cars, calmly telling the passengers, "Please step up the hillside as quickly as possible," and refusing to discuss the order further.

A few moments later the 40-foot wall of water was bearing down on the East Conemaugh yards, blotting out the horizon.

The Reverend T. H. Robinson, professor at the Western Theological Seminary in Allegheny, had been keeping a diary of the day's events for his wife. Later he filled in the following entry, "All at once a shrill long whistle sounded from an engine near by. Everyone wanted to know what it meant. I said to a lady sitting near me, 'I presume there is no danger,' but looking out of my car window I saw a

The Dam Breaks

huge mass of trees and flood-wood and water, about 200 or 300 feet away, moving toward the train."

The fact didn't register until later, but that onrushing wall of water actually didn't move as swiftly as one might imagine. Even those still in the cars when it was several hundred yards away, or less, had time to scramble up the nearby hillside, if they were fairly agile. The trouble was, many of the passengers were numbed with panic at the sight of that flood-wall.

According to Conductor Bell's report, "We hardly had time to notify the passengers, and they nearly all fled up the hillside." Bell meant all those who managed to save themselves; the majority didn't. "One old man, who with his son returned for some reason, was drowned. Two cars went down in the current. I do not know how many were drowned. The water set fire to a lot of lime and the fire caught two Pullman cars, which were destroyed, but no person was burned, the passengers all having left the train before the cars caught." (Quoted in the Philadelphia *Press* of June 3, 1889.) Actually there was only one Pullman on the train and by no means all the passengers managed to escape before the cars were engulfed. Thirty-seven passengers and crew members were listed as dead.

Mrs. Farney Tarbell, a 32-year-old woman from Cleveland, was encumbered by her three small children, Grace, seven, Bertie, five, and Howard, two. She herded them frantically toward the hill, but the flood swept over them before they could reach safety. The children's bodies were never recovered.

Jennie Paulson and Elizabeth Bryan, the 20-year-old girls bound for a Philadelphia house party, were among the first passengers to heed Conductor Bell's warning and start for the hillside. Once outside the Pullman, Jennie caught at

Johnstown

her friend's arm, staring in dismay at the dirty water swirling around her new white kid shoes.

The girls went back into the Pullman for Jennie's overshoes and were just descending the platform steps when the flood struck the car. Many days later and many miles downstream their bodies were recovered. Jennie had her overshoes on.

Dr. George M. Graham, a physician from Port Royal, Pennsylvania, had just negotiated a wide ditch, with four or five feet of water running in it, and was about to dash up the hillside when he heard screams from behind him. Nine girls and women were "struggling in the ditch with water up to their armpits. I instantly grabbed the hand of the first and quickly pulled her out. All the others reached for me at once. I succeeded in saving them all except one old lady. I said to her, 'Give me your hand—quick!' She evidently was bewildered, for she replied, 'I will go this way' and, walking toward the maddened waters, she was lost."

Dr. Robinson, the theologian from Allegheny, scrambled to safety on the hillside and then turned around to look back. "What an awful sight presented itself; houses falling and sweeping downstream; some six or eight rods away two men were dragging a woman with all their might; one car broken loose and going downstream in plunging water, two men on top, others inside. It was awful to see the men as the car rolled from side to side trying to keep on top. Then all the trains started down the river. I cried out in anguish, 'They are gone!' They went about 500 feet, and were stopped very strangely, our engine being lifted up and flung upon the head of the other train. Engines from the roundhouse were rolled down against it, a mass of trees was lodged there and a breakwater formed . . . The whole four trains, save two or three cars, were thus held in the midst of the flood."

The ditch between the railroad tracks and the hump-backed hill was a death trap for half a dozen of the passengers. According to the railroad's report, "An old millrace, never filled up, was in the way with narrow planks for cross-ings. Some of the terrified passengers jumped or fell into the waters and drowned, the deluge overtaking them as they floundered in the ditch."

The newlywed Richwoods had the most frightening ex-perience of all the survivors from the Day Express, who numbered only about a dozen. When they heard the whis-tle on Hess' engine, Richwood hurried out to the platform. Up the valley he "beheld a seething, turbulent wall of water, whose crests seemed mountain-high, filling the entire valley and carrying everything before it as cornstalks before a gale." A moment later the first plunging wave snatched up the Pullman.

"With one hand I grasped my wife around the waist, and with the other held onto the window casing like grim death, vainly trying to resist the terrible rush of water which in-stantly filled the car. Through this opening I had the pres-ence of mind to force my wife, whom I immediately fol-lowed, and we at once found ourselves making the most dizzy and fantastic convolutions in our struggle up to the surface.

"Up, and up, and up we went. We were drawn upon the floating body of a car, perhaps our own sleeper, now con-taining three persons, two men and one woman . . ."

Mrs. Richwood appeared to be unconscious, or nearly so, and her husband hurriedly set about trying to revive her and at the same time hold onto their precarious refuge atop the spinning, ricocheting railway car. In the bucking current other objects were hurled against the car, almost knocking them loose. Huge tree trunks battered at them, and other railroad cars, floating roofs, machinery, dead livestock and bridge timbers. Edith's eyelids fluttered a little and she regained consciousness. They clung to each other, expecting to be thrown back into the flood at any moment.

Then "the car crashed against some obstruction and we were thrown off. But here again Providence intervened and we were soon assisted upon a large float containing about twenty persons. Some there were with crushed and mangled limbs, others bruised, torn, and almost naked.

"We were fast approaching the north bank [where it flowed between the boroughs of Conemaugh and Woodvale]. Now directly in our path lay an immense structure, which proved to be part of the great steel manufactory [the Gautier wireworks], containing tons upon tons of molten metal, and from whose cupolas issued an awful hissing of steam, mingled with huge volumes of water as from the crater of some volcano . . ."

Richwood related that he saw scalded workmen floundering to the surface, then sinking to their deaths, and realized that he and his wife were being carried to a more agonizing ordeal than drowning. They caught a plank floating past and pushed away from the raft, kicking their legs as a means of propulsion. They never learned what happened to those who chose to stay on the raft as it drifted toward the cauldron formed by the Gautier works and its ruptured boilers and shattered furnaces.

"Clinging to each other, with our light float between us, we now heard ourselves being encouraged by those on the bank who had witnessed our desperate struggle. As we passed a point some fifty feet from shore we saw one of those sturdy fellows, stripped to the waist, plunge into the water, and with long, swift strokes succeed in reaching us. With untiring efforts, in which I was unfortunately too weak to assist, our deliverer succeeded in drawing us to shore, where willing hands tenderly cared for us."

The flood tossed locomotives around like so many bobbing corks and swept the East Conemaugh yards of the Pennsylvania as clean as a bowling alley. The 16-stall roundhouse and nine heavy engines under repair were carried downstream, along with hundreds of other cars, locomotives and rolling stock, and rails, ties, buildings and sheds full of equipment. The baggage car of the mail train broke loose from its couplings and carried thousands of letters and parcels downstream.

A few of the locomotives were on the sidings far enough from the main force of the flood to resist its massive thrust. Locomotive No. 1309, a 50-ton eight-wheeler, was found a day or two later, still on its tracks, smoke curling out of its stack and steam whistling out of its safety valve. Driftwood was heaped around it to the level of its unbroken headlight, so tightly matted that a crew worked on it all day without breaking off its cocoon. Otherwise, it was ready to chug down the tracks. Another locomotive, No. 477, had been abandoned by Engineer Henry as the flood curled up around its driving shafts. The engineer made it safely to the hillside. His locomotive was also found upright on the tracks and buried under a mass of wreckage. There were plentiful examples of the tremendous force that had gathered behind the flood. It drove the stud bolts almost through the brass number plate on Engine No. 1019. It hurled a boxcar through the wall of the Brethren Church on Somerset street, and bore the Pennsylvania Railroad's office safe from East Conemaugh to Millville.

The freight train which had been shunted between the

two sections of the Day Express was broken up and its cars scattered. A cargo of lime in one of the cars caught fire after being slaked with floodwater, and set two passenger cars aflame. They burned right down to the wheels despite the floodwater swirling around them.

The casualties among the hundreds of railroad employes working in the yards and their families at home in the borough of East Conemaugh undoubtedly would have been much greater, had not Engineer Hess tied down his whistle and raced down the valley from Mineral Point in advance of the flood.

The flood next fell upon the borough of Woodvale with its full and devastating weight. Sweeping around a bend in the Little Conemaugh, the mass of water rolled over the borough like a steamroller crushing a cardboard toy village. Except for one section in the borough of Johnstown, Woodvale suffered a heavier loss of life and property than any other community in the drowned valley. It was largely a residential area, Cambria Iron's woolen and flour mills being the only local industries. Maple avenue, bowered with shade trees, was considered the most beautiful street in all the boroughs.

Woodvale's casualty rate was particularly high because so many people were caught in their houses by the flood wave, according to Charles B. Clark, compiler of the Johnstown City Directory. "Some of them, hearing the noise, attempted to run to the hills, forty to sixty rods distant, but not many succeeded in reaching a place of safety, as the water was already too deep for rapid running; and what added to the horror of the situation, a train of freight cars was standing between them and the hill. These cars started to move with the flood, and thus many perished just at the portal of safety."

Virtually every house and shop in Woodvale was flattened by the flood or carried off downstream. All that was left standing were a stubbornly resisting fragment of the woolen mill and one wall of the flour mill.

A few of the citizens saw the flood strike the Gautier wireworks with infernal effects, exploding boilers and geysers of steam. One witness said later, "It seemed as if the whole works arose and moved forward on the water slide, as the whole came down the valley."

Frank Traut, who was on his way to report for the night shift at the railroad yards over in East Conemaugh, was caught by the flood near the ticket gate at the entrance of the fairgrounds. He was nimble both mentally and physically. Traut scrambled to the roof of the ticket office. When that was torn from its foundation, he swung himself over to a telephone pole. The force of the water was so great that it snapped off the pole, but not before Traut leaped onto a log careening downstream. Traut clung to the log for a distance of two miles, reached a mountain of wreckage and climbed over it to a safer refuge.

In its 14-mile sweep of the Little Conemaugh valley, the flood had picked up so much debris that it was practically "a moving dam driven along by the thrust of the water behind it." Yet, in a sense, this was a blessing because it choked the speed of the deluge and gave many persons time to take refuge on higher ground; every place where the valley walls grew narrower "it would jam up so tightly that for a moment the mass would cease to move," according to the study made by Professor McMaster. The temporary halts and pauses "go far to explain the slow progress of the flood."

The theoretical velocity of such a mass of water, Professor

McMaster calculated, was more than 60 miles per hour. "Even allowing for friction," he stated, the distance from the dam to the borough of Johnstown "ought to have been traversed in 25 minutes." Instead it took almost exactly an hour.

A partial inventory of the wreckage hurled upon Johnstown by the flood would include the following items:

The woodworking, woolen and flour mills of the Cambria Iron Company.

The viaduct and several bridges between South Fork and Johnstown.

The Gautier wireworks and its massive furnaces, boilers and other heavy machinery.

Two hundred huge reels of steel cable and wire weighing more than 200,000 pounds.

The roundhouse and other buildings in the East Conemaugh yards of the Pennsylvania Railroad.

Thirty-three locomotives, weighing from 50 to 85 tons each.

Eighteen passenger cars and 315 freight cars.

Hundreds of tons of pig iron.

An estimated 50 miles of railroad track.

Brick, stone, mortar and timber from hundreds of smashed houses.

Telegraph poles and wire between South Fork and Johnstown.

Parts of the wrecked dam.

Various types of farm machinery from the valley holdings.

Horses, cattle and human beings . . .

Thus the first gigantic wave of the flood was a battering ram of iron, steel, masonry, wood, human and animal flesh.

Actually, the flood had divided into two prongs before descending upon Johnstown. The Gautier works had split the flood front into two thundering torrents. One followed the channel of the Little Conemaugh toward the Stone Bridge. The other went charging up Jackson, Clinton and Franklin streets to an uproarious union with the Stonycreek above the confluence of the rivers.

It was 4:10 P.M. when the waters of the South Fork reservoir washed over the already inundated city.

5. The Flood Strikes

At 4:10 P.M. the bolt of water from the South Fork reservoir struck Johnstown, just as some residents were getting ready to move their furniture back downstairs, recover their milk cows from hillside barns, and revert from the rowboat and the raft to the horse and buggy as a means of transportation. The rain was still coming down steadily, but the black clouds were yielding to gray. There was no warning that the boroughs up the Little Conemaugh had been flattened and washed away, except for the brief blast of factory whistles and the running shriek of a train whistle.

It took just ten minutes for the waters of Conemaugh Lake to drown the city.

One of the most clear-sighted descriptions of that spectacle was furnished the New York *Sun* by a man who had watched it from the crest of Johnstown Hill:

In an instant the deserted street became black with people running for their lives. An instant later the flood came and licked them up with one eager and ferocious lap. The whole city was one surging and whirling mass of water, which swept away house after house with a rapidity that even the eye could not follow. The course of the flood was as unreasoning as the freaks of a madman and as cunningly

96

The Flood Strikes

devised as the blows of an armed maniac running amuck. A part of the wave seemed disposed to follow the course of the stream while the other part was intent upon dashing into and through the heart of the town. The conflicting forces of the element, however, kept together until the point between Franklin and Market streets was reached. Here they separated, one current sweeping along the course of the Conemaugh to the Pennsylvania Railroad bridge and the other making the dash through the town. Thus the flood had two prongs, one as destructive as the other.

Another witness with a good observation post was George C. Gibbs, assistant editor of the Johnstown *Tribune*, who was watching from the second-floor window of the newspaper building and writing a running account of the flood. "The first appearance," he wrote, "was like that of a great fire, the dust it raised. It came like a thief, and was upon us before we were aware . . . Conemaugh Borough was shaved off as if by the sharp surface of an avalanche; in a moment more Johnstown was tumbling all over itself, houses at one end nodded to houses at the other and went like a swift deceitful friend to meet, embrace and crush them. Then on sped the wreck in a swirl, the angry water, baffled for a moment, running uphill with the town and the helpless multitude on its back, the flood shaking with rage and dropping here and there a portion of its burden—crushing, grinding, pulverizing all. Then back, with great frame buildings floating along like ocean steamers, upper decks crowded, hands clinging to every support that could be reached, and so on down to the great Stone Bridge, where the houses, piled mountain high, took fire and burned with all the fury of the hell you read about—cremation alive in your own home, perhaps a mile from its foundation; dear ones slowly consumed before your eyes, and the same fate your own a moment later!

"But the flood had not yet done all its work. Cambria City remained to be destroyed, and the railroad town below if it could reach them. Cambria went like a child wipes out a pictured village on its slate, then on the waters flew. But soon they were out of the mountains and away from home, and then, as if repenting the last blow struck, the cruel current weakened and spread and all was over. . . ."

These were among the more graphic descriptions of the panoramic picture of the disaster.

To most people the flood was simply a desperate close-up; the sudden and overwhelming rush of water, the quick scramble for a refuge or the split-second grab for a piece of wreckage to keep afloat on raging waters, the agonizing struggle to keep one's head above the surface, the wild careening ride down the valley, a hand stretched out from some more stable fragment of the wreck and scatter of the city. Death, or survival, was a matter of seconds for most. For those who survived, that splinter of time would be the most vivid moment they ever experienced.

Sixteen-year-old Victor Heiser had watched the floodwaters creep up Washington street outside his home all that day, whenever he could steal time from his books. School was out for most of his fellows but, as he wrote later, "my education was forced beyond my years." He was the only son of Mr. and Mrs. George Heiser, and his father, a 50-year-old veteran of the Civil War, had a stern Teutonic sense of paternal duty. Victor was going to amount to something, Victor would not disappear into the sweat and glare of the Cambria Iron Company's mills, the destiny of most of his schoolmates. So, as unwilling a scholar as most healthy

The Flood Strikes

boys of his age, he attended public school in the daytime and learned French and German at night with a tutor. Most of the summertime was spent at a private school. He was allowed to spend one month out of the year on a farm as the "sole concession to leisure."

In the rainy darkness of late afternoon Victor was ordered by his father to look after the family's fine pair of carriage horses. The stable was on higher ground than the house, but the senior Heiser believed they should be taken to a nearby hillside for the night.

The boy had just taken the horses from their stalls and was leading them out of the stable at the rear of the house when "my ears were stunned by the most terrifying noise I had ever heard in my sixteen years of life. The dreadful roar was punctuated with a succession of tremendous crashes."

Victor glanced up at the second-floor windows of his home, where his father and mother were standing. It was his last living glimpse of them. His father motioned violently, signaling him to climb up to the red tin roof of the stable. And it was the boy's long training in absolute obedience, as it developed, that saved his life.

He clambered up to the roof of the stable only a moment before the flood hit Washington street. "From my perch I could see a huge wall advancing with incredible rapidity down the diagonal street . . . As this wall struck Washington street broadside, my boyhood home was crushed like an eggshell before my eyes, and I saw it disappear."

The stable on which he perched was able to resist the flood for only a few moments before it was ripped from its foundation and began rolling over and over like a barrel on the flood tide. "Stumbling, crawling and racing, I somehow managed to keep on top," he wrote later, and then jumped to the roof of a neighbor's house just as it and the stable were about to collide. The neighbor's house groaned and creaked under the pressure of the floodwater. Just as it was about to collapse in this hydraulic embrace, Victor leaped to another house which was more stoutly constructed. "For years thereafter I was visited by recurring dreams in which I have lived over and over again the fearful experience of hanging with my fingernails dug deep into the water-softened shingles, knowing that in the end I must let go." When he did let go, he landed back on the roof of the Heiser stable by one of those freaks of chance in which the flood abounded.

From the whirling rooftop, as it tore downstream toward the Stone Bridge, Victor saw his friends and neighbors go to their deaths with all the irrelevant and often grotesque effects that did not seem to belong in the midst of tragedy. He saw Mussante, the Italian fruit dealer, his wife and two children, racing along on "what seemed to be their old barn door." There was a Saratoga trunk open beside them and the Mussantes were frantically packing their possessions into it, oblivious of the terror around them, as if they were hurrying to catch an excursion train. Suddenly a mass of wreckage heaved up out of the thrashing waters and "they were crushed out of existence." Victor saw the stoutish Mrs. Fenn, his neighbor, "astride an unstable tar barrel which had covered her with its contents." He saw Dr. Lee's Negro hostler shivering on the roof of his master's house.

The shattered stable was passing a two-and-one-half-story brick house when Victor decided to seek a more promising refuge and leaped for its roof, where a small group of people were standing.

Victor Heiser was safe, for the time being. He had looked at his watch a moment before the flood struck, when it was exactly 4:10 P.M. Already possessed of something of the detachment of the scientist, he looked at his watch again. "It was not yet 4:30; 3,000 [sic] human beings had been wiped out in less than ten minutes."

Several blocks away from the Heiser home, at Jackson and Main, James Quinn paced up and down his porch, occasionally pausing to stare up the valley. He was one of the few men in Johnstown who seemed to have been actively concerned over the possibility that the South Fork dam would break. His wife was visiting her sister in a nearby town, and the responsibility of caring for his four daughters, his 16-year-old son, a sister-in-law, her infant son and the several servants was weighing heavily on him. His infant daughter Marie had the measles and could not be moved except as a matter of urgent necessity. His son, Vincent, was downtown helping an uncle move goods from his flooded store, but the rest of the family was at home. Quinn had already laid plans for a quick evacuation of his stout brick house. The whole household was to dash up Green Hill, rising behind the Quinn home, in case of a greater disaster than his neighbors anticipated. One of his subsidiary worries was the attitude of his sister-in-law, Mrs. Abbie Ludes, who was visiting from Kansas and had little conception of what a flood could do; she persisted in scoffing at his fears and proclaiming that "this big house would never go."

He paused to look westward again: the horizon seemed to be trembling. The dam! He was certain that his worst fears had been realized. "He looked out and saw a blur," his daughter Gertrude wrote many years later, "an advance guard, as if it were of mist, like dust that precedes a cavalry charge; and heard at the same time an ominous sound that froze the marrow of his bones . . ."

Johnstown

Quinn ran into the house, shouting, "Follow me to the hill!"

Mrs. Ludes stared at him as if wondering whether this was a joke. He shouted at her, "Follow me! Don't stop for anything! Run for your lives!"

The children's nurse, Mary Libby, screamed, "The baby with the measles!" Gertrude Quinn's infant sister, Marie, was in the darkened nursery on the third floor. Quinn dashed upstairs after his youngest daughter.

When he returned downstairs with Marie bundled in his arms, Gertrude's other two sisters, Helen and Rosemary, grabbed their father's coattails and followed him out the door.

Eight-year-old Gertrude, who worshiped her father but always seemed to be tomboyishly doing something to dismay him, tried to follow him along with her sisters. Unfortunately her Aunt Abbie, who had her two-year-old son Richard in her arms, and Nurse Libby appointed themselves Gertrude's protectors. The towheaded little girl kicked and screamed in her struggle to join her father and sisters, but the two women held on to her.

Aunt Abbie looked out at the waves of floodwater washing up Jackson street and announced, "I do not like to put my feet in dirty water."

"Mr. Quinn said we were to follow him up Green Hill," the nurse reminded Mrs. Ludes.

"This house is safer than any hillside," Mrs. Ludes proclaimed. "It will stand against any amount of water. We'll go up to the nursery and stay dry and cozy while the others are out in the rain."

Gertrude, her aunt and infant cousin and the nurse took refuge on the third floor. They looked out the windows slotted in the mansard roof. For the moment it appeared

102

The Flood Strikes

that they were better off than the panicky mob struggling up Green Hill. This was what Gertrude saw and heard as she recalled in later life:

"Screams, cries and people running; their white faces like death masks; parents dragging children; a wagon loaded to the breaking point lost a wheel and its passengers were dumped into the filthy water. Bells were ringing, the whistles in the mills were sounding a last warning and steam engines opened their throttles for the last time . . ."

A great wave rushed upon the house, rooftop-high, carrying roofs, rafters, shattered timbers, trees and furniture.

The women realized now that they should have obeyed James Quinn, knew they were trapped in a house about to be crushed by the flood.

"This is the end of the world," Aunt Abbie said, falling to her knees with her infant son in her arms. Richard was still sleeping, and would never know what cut off his young life. "We'll all die together," Aunt Abbie said with a calm acceptance.

The women began praying, and Gertrude knelt beside them, less fatalistically resigned to losing her life.

A moment later the house was engulfed; a great shudder passed through it, as it rocked on its foundations; dust and plaster fell on the kneeling figures. Water roared in as the seams of the house were split open. Gertrude stopped praying and decided to do something about saving her life.

There was a break in one of the walls under the gables through which daylight showed. Gertrude, "having been a prize climber in our orchard," to her father's former displeasure, swung herself up on a rafter and sailed through the break in the woodwork like an acrobat. Outside, fortunately, she landed on a raft of debris topped by a muddy mattress and bedding. The raft kept tilting as it bucked into the stormy current from the Stonycreek, meeting a prong of the flood, and Gertrude had to jump from side to side to keep it from capsizing.

The raft struck a dead and bloated horse, but a moment later a tree came racing along and dislodged the horse, which went bobbing out of sight "like a rockinghorse on a merry-go-round."

Gertrude had been too busy keeping the raft afloat to take stock of her situation, and now that she had a moment to think, the desolation of her position overcame her. She had never seen a dead person, and now corpses were all around her. The living were not disposed to be of much more help. She saw a little white house floating by with a man clinging to its chimney. She shouted to him for help but he chose to ignore her. In the former security of her world, she had only to appeal to a grown-up and help was forthcoming. In the nightmare which had replaced it, she had to fight alone for her life. All she could do was wail after the man who ignored her cries, "Oh, you terrible man." She noticed, too, that most of her clothing had been torn from her, all except her pantywaist.

It was getting darker and her raft kept swinging around in circles, aimlessly, caught in the backwash of the meeting of the Stonycreek and the Little Conemaugh.

Across the water she saw the old Arcade Building careening along on a fresher current. It looked like Noah's Ark with a score of people clinging to its roof.

Again she called out for help. She saw a man edge his way along the roof and prepare to plunge into the whirling waters. The others tried to prevent him from going to her rescue, and she heard him demand scornfully, "Do you think an angel from Heaven is coming down to help her?"

She saw the man leap into the water and start swimming

toward her, several times disappearing from view as a wave rolled over him. Finally he bobbed up at the edge of her raft and climbed over the side. He was a sturdy millworker named Maxwell McAchren, a dark-haired young fellow with a mustache, a strong jaw and a squarish face.

Ever after, when Gertrude tried to imagine what her personal guardian angel would look like, the angel had the square Scottish face of Max McAchren . . .

With a great bound the floodwaters washed over St. John's Roman Catholic and the German Lutheran churches at Jackson and Locust streets. Also destroyed were St. Mark's Episcopal, the Welsh Baptist, the Welsh Congregational and the German Reformed churches. Near St. John's stood the convent which sheltered the 13 nuns who taught in the parish school up the street. They hurried up to the second floor when the flood struck, and Sister Ignatia, who was in charge of the convent, clasped her crucifix and prayed. Somehow the flood spared their building, and all the sisters survived to be of great assistance in caring for the hundreds of injured and sick . . .

Mrs. Leudie Masterson, in her home near Vine and Market streets, had been watching the waters rise around her all that day. She was a newcomer and it was all rather exciting. Later she admitted, "I almost enjoyed it, as it was my first experience of the kind." Her husband came home at noon and stayed there, to her everlasting gratitude.

Late in the afternoon the Mastersons were leaning out their second-floor windows and talking to their neighbors, the Whites, and their son-in-law, a man named Delaney.

They heard a thunderous noise up the valley, and "Mr. Masterson called to Mr. Delaney that there must have been a terrible explosion up the river, for the water coming looked like a cloud of the blackest smoke I ever saw," Mrs. Masterson related. Delaney started to reply, when the crest of the flood hit the neighborhood. The White home was lifted up and turned upside down as if by a giant hand. Six of the 12 persons in the house were killed.

"My husband took our little girl in his arms, and we ran to the attic, the water following us up the stairs. I cannot say when our house was carried away, for I was not conscious that it had moved until I saw that we were just back of the Market street schoolhouse. Our house must have turned several times for we were bound very securely with telegraph and electric light wires, which I think helped to keep it from overturning as all the houses about us had."

The Mastersons rescued 27 persons in the next few hours, crowding them into their attic. One of them was their mailman, Joseph Hipp, who had been swept down from his home in the borough of Conemaugh.

Horace Rose, his wife, three sons and daughter were drinking coffee out of tin cups on the second floor of their house out on Main street. The attorney's wife, Margaret, and their daughter, June, had prepared the coffee in the fireplace of one of the bedrooms, and the family, fearing nothing worse than the usual spring inconveniences, was in a holiday mood.

The family chitchat was suddenly interrupted by a medley of sounds from the outside, "loud screams, the breaking of timbers, the alarm of a bell and the loud scream of a steam whistle." The senior Rose rushed to a window which commanded a view of the valley extending for miles. "I saw stretching from hill to hill a great mass of timber, trees, roofs and debris of every sort, rapidly advancing toward me, wrecking and carrying everything before it. It was then in the midst of the Gautier works. A dense cloud hung over the line of the rolling debris, which I then supposed was the steam and soot which had arisen from the hundreds of fires in the Gautier works as the waves rolled over them. I stood and looked as the resistless tide moved on and saw brick buildings crushed in and instantly dashed from sight, while frame tenements were quickly smashed to atoms."

White-faced, stunned and shaking with the horror of the spectacle, Rose turned and informed his family that a great flood wave was approaching and the city appeared to be doomed. Although one of the best informed men in the city, a former district attorney and state legislator, Rose even then did not connect the gigantic wave with a break in the South Fork dam.

But he understood the significance of that wave, and quietly told his family, "This means death to us all."

"Won't our big house stand against it?" asked Mrs. Rose. The women, particularly, who lived in Johnstown's spacious brick and stone houses were convinced that their homes were invulnerable to any disaster. It was inconceivable that anything could shatter the world in which they had found security, emotional and physical, since their earliest memories.

"No, Maggie," her husband said, "no building can stand against that awful jam . . . We are all lost. . . ."

The juggernaut struck the whole neighborhood a devastating blow. The nearby home of John Dibert, the banker and one of Rose's closest friends, was torn apart in a matter of seconds, killing Dibert and all members of his family except his wife, who was seriously injured.

Cracking as quickly as a matchbox under a heel, the Rose home also fell victim to the flood. Rose was caught under failing timbers and his right side was crushed. His right collarbone and shoulder-blade were fractured, several ribs were broken and their splintered edges were pressed into his lung, and patches of skin were torn from his face. Somehow Rose managed to haul himself onto the slate roof of his shattered home as it started its erratic journey down the valley. His wife and daughter were sucked into the center of a whirlpool, and were saved only after his son Winter dove into the maelstrom and hauled them to the surface. Horace Jr. had simply disappeared.

Not much more than half alive, the Rose family floated toward the Stone Bridge on the thick scum of debris.

The Reverend D. M. Miller, pastor of the Conemaugh Presbyterian Church, and his wife were on the second floor of their home at 94 Vine street in Johnstown when they saw "buildings suddenly rising from their foundations and floating toward us, crushing fences, shade and fruit trees, and telephone and electric-light poles."

In a few seconds their bedroom was waist-deep in water. Mrs. Miller jumped on the bed, which a moment later rose to the ceiling as if propelled by a hydraulic lift. At the same moment Reverend Miller leaped out a window, around which floodwaters were eddying. The minister smashed one sash of the window closest his wife, trapped inside the flooded bedroom. His arm was severely gashed but he managed to haul Mrs. Miller outside. They clung to the eaves. Mrs. Miller's strength suddenly gave out, her grip loosened, and she sank below the surface of the waters. A moment later the water bubbled up and she was thrown to the surface with a mass of debris. This time her husband took a firm grip on her. Drawn into the current of the Stonycreek, they raced down toward the tumult at The Point. Luckily, however, a backlashing current slammed their house against the flank of Westmont Hill, which rose 450 feet over the banks of the Stonycreek, and they were slowly washed back from the confluence of the rivers.

In calmer waters, they found that two of their neighbors had taken refuge on their roof, Price Davis and John Hennecamp, who had not realized their host and hostess were clinging to the eaves. The two men helped them onto the roof. All night, in their drenched clothing, they huddled together on the rooftop, fearful that the continuing rain and another rise on the river would again send them spinning down toward The Point. Two other human forms lay near by—the bodies of Hennecamp's wife and only child.

Another clergyman's wife, Mrs. Agnes Chapman, learned of the flood's approach when her husband dashed out of his study, where he had been preparing his Sunday sermon, the regular Friday afternoon chore of all the Johnstown clergy. The Reverend H. L. Chapman gasped, "There's a wave as high as this house coming down upon us!" Then the pastor of the Methodist Episcopal Church ran back into his study and turned off the natural-gas grate in his fireplace. The fear of a natural-gas explosion was stronger among many persons in Johnstown than of any amount of flooding.

With their seven-year-old granddaughter Nellie and Mrs. Brinkley, a widowed neighbor, they hurried up the stairs to the second floor and then into the attic, the water rushing up the stairs behind them. There was a grinding sound as the porches were torn loose from the structure, and the Chapmans believed the house itself was collapsing. Actually, it was determined later, the house was protected from the full impact of the flood by the walls of the adjacent church.

Johnstown

They were besieged by 18 feet of water "all around us and under us." Four persons were washed into the second floor of their house and came up the stairs to join them.

When the worst of the flood appeared to be over, Mrs. Brinkley asked Reverend Chapman to "look out and see if my house is still standing, and if it isn't just don't say anything."

The minister looked out, said nothing.

His granddaughter Nellie also peered out and could not be restrained from giving a full report: "Yes, Mrs. Brinkley, your house is gone—your house is gone."

Many of the city's most stalwart-looking buildings quickly succumbed to the flood, which cut a three-block swath through the heart of the city along Main street. Frail-looking frame houses simply rose from their foundations and joined the procession down the valley. Brick buildings crumbled. Masonry cracked after a moment's futile resistance. The YMCA Hall, the municipal buildings and other stone structures were swept away, also the principal hotels around Clinton and Main streets. Yet the wooden Millville schoolhouse, located only 300 feet above the great grinding jam of debris at the Stone Bridge, survived all assaults of the flood. Many of the victims lost their lives because they sought shelter in the buildings which looked the strongest, but happened to be in the path of the main force of the flood and collapsed in a shower of rubble rather than floating off with the irresistible flood tide. They would have stood a better chance if they had stayed in their homes, which, in many cases, drifted to the safety of the hillsides once the flood had spent itself.

The flood could be whimsically merciful, and it could be

The Flood Strikes

freakishly, almost playfully cruel. One of its most ruthless blows was reserved for a large and happy family that lived on Locust street: John Fenn, his wife and seven children. John Fenn worked 15 hours a day in his small hardware and tin-goods store on Main street to support his brood, which added a new member every 18 months with calendar-like regularity. At 35, he looked older than his age, bent, wispy-haired, often weary and harassed—but a contented man.

Fenn was hurrying home when the flood wave struck the city. His wife was watching from the second floor of their home as it overtook him. A few seconds later the house was smashed to kindling, and Mrs. Fenn found herself and her seven children clinging to the edge of their roof, which was rocking and plunging downstream.

One by one, the children were washed off the roof and drowned—Daisy . . . John . . . Virginia . . . Genevieve . . . George . . . Bismarck . . . Francis.

Each time she made a move to save one, the flood would boil up and snatch another child.

Then there was nobody left on the roof but herself. She whirled around on the impromptu raft almost demented with shock and grief. It was she whom Victor Heiser had seen whirling downstream on a barrel, her face and body covered with tar.

Mrs. Fenn was carried three miles down the flooded valley. Rescuers grappled for her raft and hauled her ashore. Still in shock, she told them quite calmly what had happened to her and her family. Suddenly the reality of her loss penetrated the artificial calm and she wailed:

"My God, what have I to live for?"

Young Dix Tittle and his family, among the few with enough foresight to flee to the hills hours in advance of the

111

disaster, had a perfect view of the destruction of Johnstown. Far below they could see the waters thunder over the intersection of Broad and Portage streets, where an aunt, uncle and cousin lost their lives, as they later learned. The spectacle was so awesome, Dix recalled in after years, that "many people thought the end of the world had come and prayed fervently."

The dramatic leap Conemaugh Lake took down the mountain valley was indeed accompanied by apocalyptic effects. "We heard a roar and then a terrific rush of air which snapped off trees from six to eight inches in diameter standing in the streets. Behind this moving wall of air came the water, thousands of tons of it, bearing muddy debris and many bodies."

They saw the wooden structure of the Eureka Skating Rink—half a block long—rise in a dowagerlike manner from its foundations and float down the valley, stately "as an ocean liner going down New York Harbor." A short time later, but out of sight, the skating rink was broken up and scattered; no trace of it was ever found.

They saw many people rushing to the roof of the new Hulbert House as the flood surrounded the building. The hotel looked impregnable, but suddenly it was crushed like an eggshell and collapsed. . . .

What the Tittles saw from a distance, the destruction of the Hulbert House, was tragic but impersonal. Close up, it was terrible. Most of the guests and a number of people who had taken shelter in the hotel, believing it was one of the strongest structures in the city—almost 60 persons altogether—were assembled in the lobby and offices. When the whistles blew the alarm, F. A. Benford, the proprietor, sent his son Walter up to the roof to find out what had happened. Walter shouted down the stairs that all he could see was a cloud of dust on the horizon and it appeared to him that Prospect Hill had just caved in.

The flood struck as most of the people were running upstairs to see the supposed cave-in.

Mrs. J. L. Smith and her three children, who had been keeping to themselves after her husband brought them there for greater safety, stayed in the lobby. A little more curiosity might have saved them. They all died very quickly as the first three floors of the brick structure collapsed and the flood poured in. Smith himself stayed at his stonecutting works down near the Stonycreek, where it was presumably much more dangerous, and survived. So did their frame house—small consolation for him—although more expensive homes in the neighborhood were swept away.

The wooden mansard roof floated free from the wreckage, and the Benfords, with a half-dozen others, did not even get their feet wet in making their escape.

One of the survivors was G. B. Hartley, of Philadelphia, who related: "When the great rush of water came, I was sitting in the parlors of the hotel. Suddenly we were startled to hear several loud shouts on the streets. These cries were accompanied by a loud crashing noise. At the first sound we rushed from the room panic-stricken.

"There was a crash and I found myself pinned down by broken boards and debris of various kinds. The next moment I felt the water surging in. I knew it went higher than my head because I felt it. The water must have passed like a flash or I would not have come out alive. After the shock I could see that the entire roof of the hotel had been carried off.

"Catching hold of something, I managed to pull myself up on the roof. The roof had slid off and lay across the street. On the roof I had a chance to observe my surroundings. Down on the extreme edge of the roof I espied the proprietor, Mr. Benford. He was nearly exhausted, and it required every effort for him to hold on to the roof.

"Cautiously advancing, I managed to creep down to where he was hanging on. I tried to pull him up, but found that I was utterly powerless. Mr. Benford was nearly as weak as myself. We did not give up, however, and in a few minutes he managed to crawl up on the roof.

"Crouching and shivering on another part of the roof were two girls, one a chambermaid of the hotel and the other a clerk in the store next to it. The clerk's arm had been torn from its socket. I took off my overcoat and gave it to her. She was in a pitiful state. A young man was caring for his mother, who had had her scalp completely torn off. He asked me to hold her head until he could make a bandage. He tore a thick strip of cloth and placed it around her head. The blood saturated it before it was well on.

"Soon after this we were rescued, more dead than alive."

Eight persons saved themselves, at least 49 lost their lives in the Hulbert House. One of the victims was a very attractive young woman whose identity was never established, nor was it determined how she came to be in the hotel. The only clue to her identity was the monogram on her clothing, "J.H.G."

Frederick Krebs, superintendent of the Gautier works, excused himself from the company of his wife and her cousin, Dr. Harriet Jones, to stroll out on the porch of his Napoleon street home in the Kernville section. It was a short street on the river flats enclosed by the loop of the Stonycreek. Floodwater was eddying around the top step of his porch. A neighbor rowing in the street in his skiff asked him, "Have you taken up your carpets yet, Fred?"

The Flood Strikes

Krebs shook his head. "When the water rises over the top step, it'll be time to take up the carpets and move the light furniture upstairs. In any event, I think the worst is over."

Krebs turned to go back into the house when another neighbor, John H. Young, yelled, "There goes Gautier!"

Hurrying to the porch rail and staring up the valley, Krebs saw that great clouds of smoke or steam were rising over the works.

He called to his wife inside the house, "Gas explosion! Turn off the gas in the grate!"

Even then it didn't occur to him that the flood had doused the Gautier furnaces and sent up those columns of steam.

A moment later he caught sight of a giant wave bearing down the valley.

Before dashing upstairs with his wife and her cousin, Krebs remembered that the maid had been nursing a toothache in the kitchen after serving dinner. He ran to the kitchen and found the poor creature with her swollen jaw, not much caring whether it was a flood or a toothache that killed her. He dragged her upstairs. His wife had remembered to snatch up their new kitten before fleeing the parlor.

The Krebs house withstood the pressure of the flood, and they saw a woman on a raft singing a hymn as she went sailing past. They watched the Pike family which lived up Napoleon street clinging to the window sills until their strength gave out. All were drowned. Wrecked houses from the upper reaches of the valley drifted into Napoleon street and by nightfall the street and the spaces between the houses were packed tightly with debris. Somehow the steeple of the Episcopal Church over on Locust street had been driven over to Napoleon street. It was the only piece of

115

wreckage they could identify from their attic window. All night the Krebses, their guest and the maid listened to the debris shifting and wedging tighter outside; it sounded like an arctic ice pack creaking and groaning in the current.

The Reverend (and Dr.) George Wagoner made his living as a dentist but his heart wasn't in the art of tooth-pulling. He was more interested in the avocation of saving souls. In his spare time he was an enthusiastic worker in the Johnstown United Brethren Church. Eventually, in recognition of his spiritual ardor, he was ordained a minister in that sect and placed in charge of the Stonycreek Mission. When the floodwaters besieged the home of the 63-year-old dentist-preacher on Market street, he and his wife, Mary, and their three daughters—Lizzie, Frances and Cora, all approaching marriageable age—whiled away the time by singing hymns. The flood wave struck and their house collapsed, killing them all.

Miss Bertha T. Caldwell, a young woman who had been teaching Mormons in Utah as part of a church mission, returned to Johnstown on leave a few days before the flood. The afternoon of May 31 she and her sister whiled away the dreary hours by writing letters in their rooms on the second floor of their home in downtown Johnstown. Their parents were on the first floor. Bertha heard the warning whistle blow but continued with her writing, not realizing the significance of the alarm. A few moments later her father bounded up the stairs and announced, "We're lost—the dam up at the South Fork reservoir has broken loose." The family quickly moved to the third floor.

Miss Caldwell looked out just in time to watch the approach of the flood's first wave. "A block away we saw a perpendicular wall of water, seemingly a mountain in height, with smoke, dust and vapor flying in all directions. It was coming right toward us. We saw a three-story brick building knocked down like a toy house. I heard something splash in our lower hall and called down, 'Is anyone drowning? Come on up here.' We expected the house would be swept away any minute.

"The house of our neighbors next door went down and the poor souls drowned before our eyes. The children screamed and stretched out their arms to us crying, 'For God's sake, help us.' Papa called back, 'God help you. We'll also be washed away in a minute.'"

The water rose up around the waists of the Caldwells, and there seemed to be nothing they could do to save themselves. "My father put his arms around us and said we would all die together." Bertha, however, was not quite so resigned to death. She floundered over to the windows and saw that the floodwater was flowing into the house through the second-floor windows, "sending a spray many feet high." Through the spray she caught sight of a rooftop below, and "believing that we would be lost if our house fell I caught hold of mother and we jumped to the roof below, calling upon my father and sister to follow."

The family crawled over housetops and masses of timber until they reached Main street, a block away, and climbed into the upper floor of a three-story building which had withstood the flood thus far. Scores of others had already gathered there, many of them separated from their families. "The town clock struck five," as Bertha Caldwell described the scene. "We still heard the shrieks of drowning people and their cries for help. Now, for the first time, I realized that I had no dress on. It must have been torn off me. I stood shivering in a skirt, wet to the waist . . ."

The flood occasionally spared the most helpless of creatures. Mr. and Mrs. Abram Mangus were alone in their house at 27 Main street when it was battered loose from its foundation by the flood. Shortly after they took refuge in the attic, the house being carried along downstream, several persons climbed inside. Suddenly, too, a naked baby drifted close to the attic window and was brought inside. Mrs. Mangus immediately wrapped him in a shirt and the child was soon revived enough to wail his displeasure. Three times the Mangus house drifted toward the burning debris jammed up behind the arches of the Stone Bridge, but each time countervailing currents pushed it back from certain destruction. Finally the Manguses and their guests were able to climb over the mounds of debris to the Union street schoolhouse. Climbing through a window of the schoolhouse, Mrs. Mangus gripped the shirt in which the baby was wrapped with her teeth and carried him inside as a cat carries a kitten. She unwrapped the child as other refugees gathered around. "That's my baby!" one of the women cried. The mother claimed him before the Manguses could even learn the name of the baby they had saved.

White-haired and handsome, the Reverend David J. Beale, pastor of the Presbyterian Church, calmly worked on the first draft of his Sunday sermon in the study of his home. It was shortly before 4 P.M. but Reverend Beale, like most of his fellow citizens, had no fear that Johnstown would be flooded any worse than usual in the spring. As he wrote later concerning his attitude, "We had no news of any apprehended danger of the bursting of the dam. Nor do I suppose that many of our citizens believed that in the event of the breaking of the reservoir it would greatly increase the volume of water at our distance from its location. When one of our leading citizens was asked at this time how much higher he thought the flood would reach if the South Fork dam would give way, his reply was, 'About two feet.'"

A few minutes after four o'clock Mrs. Beale came into the study and asked for his help in taking up the carpet in the parlor. Reverend Beale pointed out that the flood threat seemed to be decreasing. He left his sermon reluctantly and joined his wife, two sons, David and Thomas, 12 and 14 years old, and their daughter, in taking up the carpet, "contrary to my own judgment of the necessity of the case."

Then the minister returned to his study and was about to take up his pen again when he heard a sound "like that of an approaching railroad train." He looked out his study window and saw the flood wave bearing down the street.

By that time the Beales had been joined by a parishioner and his two sisters, who apparently felt safer in the presence of their pastor.

He rushed into the parlor, shouting, "Upstairs, upstairs everyone!"

Reverend Beale thought only to save the family Bible, and his daughter snatched up the canary in its cage.

By the time they all reached the second-floor landing, the water had rushed up to their waists. They went on up to the attic.

Reverend Beale, his family and the Lloyd family huddled together waiting for the crash that would plunge them all into the raging waters. In less than two minutes the water rose to their knees.

A man was washed into the attic window beside Reverend

Beale. "Who are you?" the pastor demanded in astonishment. "Where are you from?"

"Woodvale," the visitor gasped. Later he told them that his house was destroyed in the borough several miles up the valley and he had been carried downstream on a roof.

Reverend Beale led his family and guests in prayer, "expecting at any moment to be 'present with the Lord.'" Then he opened the old family Bible and read the consoling verses of the 46th Psalm:

> "God is our refuge and strength, a very present help in trouble.
>
> Therefore will not we fear, though the earth be removed, and though the mountains be carried into the midst of the sea;
>
> Though the waters thereof roar and be troubled, though the mountains shake with the swelling thereof. Selah."

The parsonage still stood firm against the pressure of the flood, but from the groans and tremors set up by the stress of its timbers Reverend Beale knew it could not last the night. A decision had to be made, and all these people looked to him to make it.

Through the attic windows they watched the wreck of the city, saw friends and parishioners go whirling to their deaths. "I recognized J. Q. A. Benshoff, our leading bookseller," wrote Reverend Beale later in *Through the Johnstown Flood* (Philadelphia, 1889), which provides the most authoritative account of how the city was relieved of its suffering; "Mrs. John Fulton and daughter, Charles Barnes, Mrs. Grace Young, and many others as they were dashed past our residence. I saw two little children, alone and almost nude, clinging to a roof as it passed by . . ." Reverend Beale spotted an old friend, Captain A. N. Hart, his wife, two children and a sister "struggling among the wreckage which had drifted near the parsonage" and with the help of the other men in the attic "succeeded in getting them into my house through a window."

There were now 15 persons in the attic, making it all the more imperative for Reverend Beale and Captain Hart to decide on evacuating the house. They could see mountains of wreckage piled up behind the Stone Bridge, and there appeared to be solid footing all the way over to Main street.

"Alma Hall is still standing," Captain Hart pointed out. The building, used mainly for lodge meeting rooms and professional men's offices, loomed over the mountainous debris. "It would be quite a climb but I think we could make it if we stick together."

The town clock tolled five o'clock and a rainy twilight was approaching.

"We haven't long to make up our minds," Reverend Beale said. "It would be too dangerous to try crossing in the dark. It's going to be hard enough as it is with the women and children. I can see open spaces we'll have to jump or bridge over with planks."

"I seriously doubt whether your house will last the night," Captain Hart said.

"Let's go, then, while there's still light," the minister said.

The debris was stacked right up to the attic windows by this time, and if the mountain-climbing party was lucky they would reach the comparative safety of Alma Hall without even getting their feet wet, literally walking over the flood. In downtown Johnstown there were 20 or more feet of water in the streets, and a layer of debris over that of a thickness varying between ten and 30 feet.

Reverend Beale helped the women and children out of the attic window and told them to keep close together. "Just

as I was about to pass David and Thomas out the window,"
he wrote later, "they expressed the desire that their dog
'Guess,' which stood by, mutely pleading for his life, should
be saved, and accordingly 'Guess' was let down upon the
roof. No sooner had he reached it than, true to doggish nature, he and a neighbor's cur engaged in an earnest and free
fight for the supremacy." Reverend Beale, his family and
friends set out for Alma Hall, "walking and jumping from
one house or roof to another, sometimes compelled to bridge
over deep watery spaces with loose boards or planks." They
left just in time, as it developed, for a short time later the
worst horror of the disaster occurred among the debris
backed up behind the Stone Bridge, and later in the night
the Beale house collapsed and sank into the waters.

6. The Fire Follows the Flood

THE STONE BRIDGE, which was 50 feet wide and accommodated the four tracks of the Pennsylvania Railroad's main line to Pittsburgh, was turned into a firm and effective, only slightly leaky, dam. It crossed the Conemaugh just below the confluence of the Little Conemaugh and the Stonycreek. Solid-footed and based on seven 58-foot stone spans, it was built to last centuries (and, in fact, still carries the Pennsylvania's main line across the Conemaugh). The flood could not even shake the Stone Bridge. Partly this was because the main body of the flood, following the channel of the Little Conemaugh, struck the Westmont hillside overlooking the confluence of the rivers and spent much of its force. It still had sufficient propulsion to shatter the borough of Millville on the other side of the Conemaugh before plunging down on the boroughs of Cambria, Morrellville, Coopersdale and Sheridan Station.

Behind the Stone Bridge, however, thousands of tons of wreckage, most of the spoils of the flood's sweep of the valley, were backed up in mounds 20 to 30 feet high, covering 30 acres. Johnstown itself was converted into a lake of filthy water. The South Fork reservoir had simply transferred itself from the mountain valley to the city below, and the Stone Bridge had become a rough approximation of the

South Fork dam. The great jam of debris consisted mostly of shattered houses, plus locomotives and railroad cars, steel tracks, hundreds of miles of steel cable and barbed wire, machinery, boulders, trees, animals and humans. It was so tightly jammed together—much of it actually bound with wire and cable into gigantic and unbreakable packages—that it later took days to tear, chop and blast traverses in the mountains of debris. To illustrate the force with which the flood rammed all this wreckage together, a steel rail found in the pile-up behind the Stone Bridge was twisted into a perfect letter "S."

Many people survived in the watery catacombs which honeycombed these ruins, trapped between crushed walls, between houses, under roofs. Once the main force of the flood had spent itself, an estimated two to three thousand persons, the living and the dead, populated this accumulation of ruins. Many extricated themselves and fled over the shaky hillocks and water-filled crevasses, reached safety within an hour after the flood struck; others were rescued by their fellow citizens.

Many more were trapped in the debris when fire broke out and burned for three days and nights. Three hundred charred bodies eventually were removed from the blackened mass of drift. It was the most horrible aspect of the Johnstown disaster.

At 5:45 P.M., about an hour and a half after the flood wave hit the city, the drift towering 15 feet above the Stone Bridge caught fire. The fire broke out in several places almost simultaneously, from live coals spilled out of a stove in a wrecked house and from a railroad car whose cargo of lime burst into flame when slaked with water. Then crude petroleum spilled from another car and gave the flames an explosive impetus. Oil-soaked bridge timbers caught fire and burned fiercely.

It was dark now, and the flames cast a lurid light over the flooded city.

Assistant Editor George Gibbs, from his still-intact vantage point on the second floor of the *Tribune* building, wrote: "Down at the bridge—what a glow it made! People were told that the wreck had been fired to clear the way, to break the jam. Well that they believed that story. St. John's Church, with a corpse in it [Gibbs referred to Mrs. Mary McNally, whose funeral services had been interrupted that morning by the rising waters], fired no one knows how, and then the houses on both sides of it. How like guards the people watched the flames, and questioned one another. 'It's going down; it's blazing up again; it's coming this way!' Calls from roof to roof, 'What's burning now?' and answers that in the stillness succeeding the first wild hours had an awful sound."

Even those out of reach could not feel safe in the flame-streaked twilight. "Their refuge was the wreckage left behind and the few buildings that, sheltered in some way, survived the shock. But all around were buildings falling. Crash succeeded crash, wild shrieks were heard on every side, and 'our turn's next' was the thought in every mind."

One of the most chillingly precise and restrained accounts, close-up, of how the fire swept the ruins backed up behind the Stone Bridge was provided by a Catholic priest, Father Trautwein, who had hurried to the scene just after the fire broke out. "A thousand persons were struggling in the ruins and imploring for God's sake to release them," he later told a New York *Sun* reporter. "Frantic husbands and fathers stood at the edge of the furnace that was slowly heating to a cherry red and incinerating human victims.

Johnstown

"Everyone was anxious to save his own relatives, and raved, and cursed, and blasphemed until the air trembled.

"No system, no organized effort to release the pent-up persons was made by those related to them. Shrieking, they would command, 'Go to that place, go get her out, for God's sake get her out,' referring to some loved one they wanted saved. Under the circumstances it was necessary to secure organization and, thinking I was trying to thwart their efforts when I ordered another point to be attacked by the rescuers, they advanced upon me, threatened to shoot me or dash me into the raging river.

"One man who was trying to steer a float upon which his wife sat on a mattress lost his hold and never again appeared. The anguish of the man was simply heart-rending. He raised his arms and screamed in his mental agony, then disappeared below the surface of the waters.

"Every effort was made to save every person who was accessible, and we have the satisfaction of knowing that fully two hundred were spared from cremation. One young woman was found under the dead body of a relative. A force of men attempted to extricate her and succeeded in releasing every limb but one leg. For three hours they labored, and every moment the flames swept nearer and nearer.

"I was on the point several times of ordering the men to chop her leg off. It would have been much better to save her life even at that loss than have her burn to death. Fortunately it was not necessary; but the young lady's escape from mutilation or death was closer than she will ever realize."

A 19-year-old girl from Millville named Rose Clark was even more gruesomely trapped in the flaming debris. The

The Fire Follows the Flood

flood had caught her on a Johnstown street and carried her downstream on some floating wreckage. Fortunately she found herself on top of the drift at the Stone Bridge after the main body of the flood had passed. Her head and torso were above water but she couldn't extricate her left leg from the crushed portion of a house in which it was caught. She saw flames spurt out of the drift an hour later but still hadn't managed to wriggle herself loose, although she could feel the floodwater swirling around her legs and knew that a sudden shift in the debris beneath her might cause her to be sucked into the waters below.

Rose had the oddest sensation that some ghostly hand was clinging to her left ankle and wouldn't let her go; it held on so tightly that her foot was benumbed.

The flames came sweeping closer to the place where she was trapped. Catching a glimpse of men moving across the smoky horizon of the burning ruins, she called out to them for help. Three men came to her rescue. One carried a small axe, another had a knife in a sheath attached to his belt. They tried to pull her out of the trap and failed, although they almost wrenched her arms out of their sockets. They hacked away at the splintered boards which held her in a viselike grip, but it was something beneath them that clutched so relentlessly. Something down in the water kept her pinned to the wreckage.

One of the men risked his life to dive into the water and explore under the ledge of the drift in which she was trapped, an operation about twice as hazardous as chopping a hole in an ice-covered lake and hoping to find one's way back to light and air and life. The man disappeared so long that his companions feared that he had been caught on a snag and drowned. But he came up a moment later, his lungs bursting and his eyes bloodshot.

127

After climbing back onto the drift and pausing to catch his breath, he told the other two men:

"Wouldn't have believed it if I hadn't seen it with my own eyes. Know what's holding on to this girl's ankle? A dead man!"

"This is no time for grisly jokes," the oldest man of the rescue party said.

"It's no joke," the swimmer said. "There's a corpse with a death grip on this girl's ankle. If you don't believe it, go down and see for yourself."

"I'll have to take your word for it," the older man said wryly.

Rose had managed to keep a grip on herself, knowing that succumbing to panic might be fatal, but now she wept openly. The fire was coming so close that she could feel its breath feverish on her face. They would have to abandon her, and she would die in the flames. What frightened her almost more than the imminence of a terrible death was the thought of dying in the clutch of that dead man. She could imagine how he had made one last desperate grab to save himself, feeling warm flesh in his hands and hoping for a fleeting instant that he might save himself, then clinging to her even as death overwhelmed him. It would be horrible, somehow obscene to die in that stranger's clasp.

"Don't leave me," Rose begged the men. "If you can't get me out, don't leave me like this. You have a knife . . ."

The older man said, "We won't leave you, girl, and that's a promise."

The man who had explored under the wreckage assured her, "I'm going back down there and cut you loose. Don't worry. I know my way this time."

Again he plunged into the water-filled crevasse, and a few moments later she could feel him working at the thing

128

Culver Service

rough this 100-yard gap the waters of Lake Conemaugh
aped and went "howling down the mountain" on Johnstown.

All that remained of Lake Conemaugh and the 20 million tons of water
impounded behind the South Fork dam. In the center background can
be seen the clubhouse of the South Fork Fishing and Hunting Club.

ational News Photos

photographic view of the surviving portion of the city

This was the 30-acre jam of wreckage behind the Stone Bridge, with the Cambria Iron Company's main works in the background.

Brown Br●

One of hundreds of dead caught in the hummocks of debris

The shattered remains of the Day Express in the
East Conemaugh yards of the Pennsylvania Railroad

A broken tower standing guard over the ruins

The wreckage of Cambria Iron's warehou

The living search for their dead on Main Street.

The height and for
of the flood wave w
illustrated by this tr
trunk hurled throu
an overturned hous

On a hillside overlook-
ing Johnstown one of
the city's surviving fam-
ilies starts life over
again.

which clung to her with an insensate fury and seemed to be saying, "If I die, you die too."

The swimmer hacked her ankle loose, and the other two men dragged her out of the wreckage. She fled with her three rescuers only a few minutes before the flames spread to the area where she had been trapped.

Another involuntary wayfarer in the drift behind the bridge was W. B. Tice, who lived with his wife over his drugstore at 31 Portage street. That morning he had moved Mrs. Tice and her pet birds to the home of friends, Mr. and Mrs. Nathan Oldham, in a higher section of Johnstown, then returned to take care of his store.

When the flood struck, Tice climbed out the window of his living quarters and swung himself up to the roof just in time to escape being overwhelmed by the first wave. In those few moments eight persons were washed up on the roof with him, "some praying, some weeping and wailing, some cursing." The store was jolted off its foundation and joined the concourse of wreckage bolting downstream toward the Stone Bridge.

The two-story building disintegrated quickly under the pressure of the floodwater, and Tice and his eight guests found themselves with nothing but the rickety roof between them and the stormy crest of the flood. It sailed about three blocks before bumping into the solider structure of the Wood, Morrell & Company store. Tice abandoned his fellow voyagers and jumped to a pile of lumber that looked more substantial. It carried him into the drift and became tightly jammed with the other debris. From his perch Tice watched "whole families of my acquaintance wiped out of existence." He heard the town clock sound five o'clock, and wondered if he would ever hear another hour strike.

Johnstown

A wild-eyed and bedraggled woman on a raft went spinning downstream and singing at the top of her voice:

> Jesus, Lover of my soul,
> Let me to Thy bosom fly,
> While the raging billows roll,
> While the tempest still is high.

Tice thought the hymn was strikingly appropriate, and was still brooding over it when several other men beckoned to him from what appeared to be dry land and showed him a safe path over the rocking and grinding debris underfoot. He touched solid ground with the most profound gratitude. A few moments later fire broke out on the drift. He later recalled:

"I went up on the embankment and looked across the bridge, which was filled with debris, and on it were thousands of men, women and children, who were screaming and yelling for help, as at this time the debris was on fire, and after each crash there was a moment of silence, and then those voices crying in vain for help. At each crash hundreds were forced under the surface of the debris."

Tice saw "hundreds of them throw up their hands and fall backward into the fire" as the flames approached, and "those who had escaped drowning were reserved for the more horrible fate of being burned to death."

When Tice "could endure it no longer," he climbed to the top of the hill where the whole panorama of the disaster was spread out before him, fire and flood, wrecked and burning houses, homeless people on the hills and others fighting for their lives on the drift before the bridge. He saw flames leap from St. John's Catholic Church. Near by was the home of the friends with whom his wife had sought refuge.

The Fire Follows the Flood

Tice couldn't see whether the house was still standing and had no idea whether his wife was alive. There was no way to find out at the moment, with one of the prongs of the flood between him and the Oldham house.

Tice wandered off to seek shelter for the night in a patch of wet woods, the few remaining homes in the vicinity already being crowded to the rafters with women and children refugees. "A more terrible and lonesome night than that alone in the woods I never spent, knowing that my friends mourned me as dead and not knowing, in fact, whether they were alive themselves."

For Tice, at least, there was a happy ending: the next day he and his wife were reunited, "happy but penniless and homeless."

J. M. Frontheiser, superintendent of one of the Cambria Iron Company's works, saw his wife and one of his daughters drown when the flood destroyed their home on Main street. He managed to save his son and his other daughter, and all three found themselves on the mound of debris stacked up behind the Stone Bridge, he later told a New York *Times* reporter.

The 12-year-old girl told her father, "Let me go, Papa, and save brother. My leg is broken and my foot is caught below."

"I won't leave either of you," Frontheiser said.

"Then get a sharp knife and cut my leg off," the girl said. "I can stand it."

His ten-year-old son said, "You can't save me either, Papa, both of my feet are caught fast and I can't hold out any longer."

Rescuers climbed over the wreckage and managed to release the two children just before the fire swept over that area.

Charles R. Phipps, an office worker, was lucky enough to escape from his home just before the floodwaters crushed it. A standing broad-jump to a floating roof carried him out of that immediate danger but he was soon caught up in the maelstrom at The Point. He abandoned the roof for the more substantial-appearing refuge of a three-story brick house, which had been abandoned by its occupants. It was less secure than Phipps had imagined. He found the floor of the bedroom on the second floor canted at a 45-degree angle; the house was sitting tipsily on its foundation, and threatened to collapse at any moment. Every time another house or barn was driven against it by the flood it tottered as if it had been built on rockers. The fire erupting from the drift near by was only an additional hazard. By that time others had crawled, dripping and exhausted apparitions, into the tottering house.

"The square above us was one raging torrent which afterward calmed and glided noiselessly by, where a few moments before there were hundreds of happy homes. The silence of this river of death was interrupted by the occasional cry of a poor human being who was being carried on its bosom to the flames a few squares below," Phipps related to a reporter.

The shivering refugees in the brick house were grateful for a little warmth, at first, when St. John's Church caught fire, but "its fierce flames were driving out those who had taken refuge within its walls and on the surrounding houses. About ten o'clock the great steeple fell after supporting a vast flame that shot high in the air, and the fine building was totally in ruins. This and the whole square that was

132

The Fire Follows the Flood

burned and the greater and more horrible fire at the Stone Bridge added a horror to the night never to be forgotten."

There were 15 persons in the house by now. Deciding it had become unsafe, they moved to a solid-looking heap of debris and pooled their efforts to make the best of a most uncomfortable night. Phipps later told a reporter:

"We managed to get hold of some floating canvas and made a little tent under which we huddled together to keep off some of the rain continually pouring down. My dog had followed me through it all, and as several of us had no shoes on, we made him lie down at our feet to keep them warm."

During the night they were awakened several times by faint cries from the honeycombed wreckage below. They investigated and found people trapped and near suffocation or drowning. All were rescued and "taken under our extemporized tent."

It was 16 hours after the flood struck before Phipps and several of the others were able to make a raft, find a pole and propel themselves to a headland of dry ground on Jackson street.

The freakish element in human nature came to the surface even under the most desperate circumstances. A rescue party working its way through the shattered houses on the drift found one unconcerned lady primping in front of the mirror in her all-but-wrecked bedroom. "Come along, ma'am," they said, "the fire will reach here any minute." She believed, however, that a lady should look her best at all times and said, "Just wait until I finish putting up my hair, gentlemen." With remarkable patience, they waited until she had finished fussing over her elaborate hairdo and stepped elegantly over her threshold as if on her way to a ball at the Cambria Club. Another team of rescuers came upon a woman sitting calmly in her roofless parlor, her hands folded in her lap, apparently oblivious to the rain pouring in on her. When they told her the fire was approaching, she said, "I think I'll just stay here." Shock had obviously deprived her of her reason, and the men carried her out of the wreck of her house. A young woman named Florence McConaughy, whose home had been located at 130 Walnut street but which was now crushed in with the debris behind the bridge, refused to leave with a rescue party even though she could see the flames advancing over the hummocks of debris. "My father is down there," she said, pointing to the mass of timbers below. "Have you heard him call out?" she was asked. "No, but he was in the house with me when the flood came, and I know he's there, and I won't leave without Pa." Realizing it was futile to argue against feminine intuition, the rescuers hurriedly began ripping into the rubble beneath them. They found that Florence was right. Her father was buried under broken timbers, motionless but still breathing, and both were rescued with only minutes to spare.

Horace Rose, the attorney, described the sensations of those who watched from a place of temporary safety as fire consumed what the flood had wrecked. A sort of threnody sounded for the whole ruined city from the Lutheran Church, which housed the town clock in its spire. "Five times the ponderous hammer struck the massive bell, tolling the dreadful knell of the thousands who had perished in that awful hour. No one can imagine the horrible sensation the slowly beating strokes of the clock sent through the floating survivors of that terrible hour."

7. The Survivors Fight for Their Lives

THICK-WALLED and invincible even under the tremendous pressure of the floodwater and the battering of the wreckage, Alma Hall still stood on its foundations at 438 Main street. To hundreds of persons in the flattened city it was a beacon in the storm, representing at least the possibility of a refuge at a time when, shocked by the merciless destruction of all their familiar surroundings, people believed the end of the world had come. Even those who couldn't reach the stout old building, three of its four stories above the water level, took encouragement from its presence. Many people risked their lives to cross the debris and seek shelter there, among them Reverend Beale, his family and fellow refugees.

It was a perilous journey over the crunching debris, Reverend Beale recalling, "We were walking and jumping from one moving house or roof or boxcar to another; sometimes we were out of sight of each other, and sometimes we were compelled to bridge over deep watery spaces with loose boards or planks. One of the young ladies, walking on a piece of scantling, fell into a watery chasm and we could see nothing but her hair floating on the surface. She was pulled up on some floating timbers."

Darkness had fallen by the time the minister's party

reached Alma Hall but "some of our number now went out on the wreckage, taking the rope we brought from the parsonage, and succeeded in extricating a number of people who were either caught in the timbers of the drift or were much too exhausted to help themselves."

Inside the hall there was safety, for the moment, but there were enough other problems to cause deep concern among the more responsible citizens. Two hundred and sixty-four persons sought shelter there the night of May 31-June 1, and not all of them were inclined to fall on their knees and thank God for having spared them. Some were intent on celebrating or drowning their sorrows with whisky. A few drunken men rampaging among defenseless women and children could have caused a panic. There was also the possibility of an explosion in one of the natural-gas mains, which could have added its horrors to fire and flood. And many, watching the rain continue to fall steadily through the night, were quite certain that another bolt of floodwater would finish off the city before dawn.

Reverend Beale wrote later that he would never forget the atmosphere of fear which drenched Alma Hall and its occupants that night, or "the howlings of terror-stricken brutes; the darkness and confusion throughout the building; the sickening and stifling odors; the horrible scenes on the wreckage about us; and the expressed opinions of contractors present that the great building would yield to the fearful strain."

Among those gathered at Alma Hall were John Fulton and his family. Fulton was the Cambria Iron Company engineer who had warned in a report to the president that the South Fork dam was not entirely safe. It was no consolation now, that his unheeded warning had proved well founded. The only consolation was that all of his family had been saved. One of his daughters was caught in the First National Bank building when the flood wave struck the city. She and a half dozen others ran up to the roof. By hopping from one roof to another just before they collapsed, Miss Fulton had reached Alma Hall. Her father, mother and sisters were driven from the second floor to the third floor to the roof of their home as the water overwhelmed it. Their rooftop whirled away but fortunately rammed into Alma Hall, and they abandoned it half a minute before it collapsed and sank. The Fultons were reunited with their daughter only a few minutes after the flood struck. Few families in the city were so fortunate.

James M. Walters, the attorney whose office was on the second floor of Alma Hall, was also the beneficiary of the flood's occasionally freakish good will. He was home with his family at 135 Walnut street when the flood rolled over the city. Walters was carried off in one part of the house while his wife and children were borne downstream on the roof (they were all reunited a few days later). Walters rode his piece of wreckage down Main street until it struck Alma Hall and threw him right through the window of his own office.

Walters too saw the necessity of a government pro-tem for the building that night. "The scenes were most agonizing. Heart-rending shrieks, sobs and moans pierced the gloomy darkness. Under the guardianship of the men all took more hope. No one slept at all during the long dark night. Many knelt for hours in prayer, their supplications mingling with the roar of the waters and the shrieks of the dying in the surrounding houses. In all this misery two women gave premature birth to children."

The only physician in the building was Dr. W. E. Matthews. He had suffered several fractured ribs when he was caught under falling timbers, but despite his injuries he worked through the night to attend the sick and hurt, the grief-stricken and hysterical.

The responsible men gathered in the building held a brief meeting and set up their one-night government. Walters was elected director of the building. Three controllers were named for each of the habitable floors—Reverend Beale, Dr. Matthews and Captain Hart. They promulgated and strictly enforced exactly two laws:

(1) All hard liquor must be surrendered to the controllers.

(2) No matches or candles were to be lit, for fear of setting off an explosion of natural gas leaking from a broken main in the basement.

The people in Alma Hall had all the best of it that night, but even they were deprived of food, drinking water, dry clothing, bedding and medical supplies. Everyone had lost his home and most of his possessions. Most had lost one or more members of their families.

Even under these desperate circumstances Reverend Beale was able to think of the next day and the problems it would bring. He remembered how Paris had been overrun by thieves and other criminals when the Prussian army marched in, almost a score of years ago. It occurred to him then that Governor Beaver must be telegraphed as soon as possible to send troops and maintain order.

The Reverend H. L. Chapman, who was among the refugees in Alma Hall, heard one woman say, "I think the Methodist Church will save us," meaning that one of the nearby churches would help bolster the building against the floodwater.

"No, no," another woman cried out, "only the Catholic Church can save!"

In a nearby building that also stood up against the flood,

The Survivors Fight for Their Lives

Bertha Caldwell, the teacher who was visiting her family from her Utah mission, sat up all night with 120 other refugees in the halls and offices with every hour "seeming as long as a day. It rained incessantly and the cries for help never ceased." That was one of the most agonizing elements of the night for those who were saved, listening to the outcries from the drift and being unable to help those trapped in the debris. Miss Caldwell and her family—who learned later that her grandmother, two aunts and three cousins had lost their lives—clung together "shivering and half dead from fright and exposure." She said later:

"I wondered if my body would be recognized when found and where I should be buried. The suspense was horrible. I heard men pray who heretofore had spoken God's name only in an oath."

It was Miss Caldwell's observation that "the women bore up better than the men" among the refugees in her building.

From his observation post in the *Tribune* building, Assistant Editor Gibbs wrote, "And then there was the darkness coming on . . . Wife, husband, children, whole families separated—no way to get news of one another, and the long hours of the night ahead. Nothing to do but sit and wait in dread, cheering others if you could, and being cheered by other souls in return—helping and being helped the whole night through.

" 'Who are you?' 'Who's with you?' and so, in the way that rumors fly, a good part of the whole day's story went, and hearts that had hoped, sank in despair, while hearts that had feared and quailed for loved ones thanked God that they were saved.

"All through the night house upon house that had partly held together after the first great crash, and had stood the awful journey down and up and down again, went to pieces

139

with its occupants, and then came heroic deeds of daring by which many were saved, and the most frightful experiences until other roofs were reached, only to be gone through again perhaps a moment later . . . Here a strong man, mangled in the wreck, passed away in the night; there women died from shock, or brought new men and women into the world in their hour of double anguish. Here lay the sick and the maimed, favorite doctor dead and no other to be had; there lay a corpse washed in by the flood, as cheerful as its company . . ."

Horace Rose, the attorney, and most of his family drifted around the backwash of the jam at the Stone Bridge as darkness fell. They heard the "dreadful knell" of the town clock striking five o'clock. Shortly thereafter they were rescued by Dr. Harry Phillips, a dentist who practiced in Pittsburgh but was visiting his native Johnstown. Dr. Phillips spotted the Roses from the home of his host, Dr. S. M. Swan, and made his way toward them over the treacherous footing of the debris, which was not as closely packed as it was closer to the Stone Bridge. The town clock was just striking six as the Roses were helped into Dr. Swan's home. The water had risen above the stained-glass windows of the Lutheran Church, which housed the dolorous bell, and a little later in the evening the structure collapsed.

The two dentists patched up the senior Rose as best they could, but he was in agony from the multiple fractures in the right side of his torso. No opiates were available and he had to suffer the whole night through, wracked not only with the pain of his injuries but the anxiety of not knowing what had happened to his sons. Winter Rose, who had saved his father's life, was with them, but 27-year-old Horace Jr., 16-year-old Forest and 14-year-old Percy were still out in the wreck of the city. They were all reunited next day. Meanwhile, the gloomy hours passed slowly. "The thousand and one alarms of the night followed; the crash of buildings was heard as they settled in the water or were crushed by the weight from above, and over all was the ghastly and lurid light that came from the burning debris at the Stone Bridge below," Rose subsequently wrote.

Young Dix Tittle and his family, among the few hundred who had sought the safety of the hillsides before the flood struck, watched the city's buildings burning weirdly above the flood waters" and the water swirling around the eaves of St. Joseph's Church on Railroad street . . . the whole incredible panorama of flood and fire working to blot out the city. Then they plowed over muddy roads until they reached the farm home of Louis Baumer, where there was still a little space available, shelter from the rain, a plate of hot food. Dix and one of his sisters slept on a cupboard shelf and the others "were sleeping wherever they could lie down, even on top of the piano."

The cheerful and competent Mrs. Leudie Masterson, whose home had been jammed into the debris behind the Market street schoolhouse, was busy looking after 27 persons who had taken shelter in her attic. Grateful that her husband and small daughter had been spared with her, Mrs. Masterson unpacked all their winter clothing and distributed it among "the poor drenched creatures who came to us." Late that night one of the women in her attic gave birth to a son, with Mrs. Masterson and the other women acting as midwives. They all agree that he must be christened Moses, remembering the biblical verse, "And she called his name Moses . . . 'Because I drew him out of the water.'"

Another Moses was among the "flood babies" born that

night. His parents, Mr. and Mrs. Griffith Williams, who had migrated to this country from Wales, lived on Conemaugh street. They were among a number of people who took refuge at the home of Mr. and Mrs. George Doerr at the intersection of Vine street and Lee place. Others of the Doerr guests included Dr. L. H. Mayer, his wife and parents, who arrived on a piece of wreckage from their own home at 163 Main street. When Mrs. Williams went into labor that night, Dr. Mayer stepped forward and took charge of the accouchement.

Two other women who gave birth that night named their sons Flood.

Mrs. Annette Raymond felt her time approaching that afternoon in her home at 269 Iron street in Minersville, below the confluence of the Little Conemaugh and the Stonycreek. She saw the flood front rip the houses of Cambria City off their foundations and feared her own would go with the rest.

Mrs. Charles Williams took her two children, Charlotte and Ralph, and despite her condition struggled with them up the hill, its slope greasy with the rain, which rose behind their house. Her husband found his family there at nightfall and told them their home had been spared. He carried his wife back down the hill and summoned a Minersville midwife. The latter arrived just in time to assist at the birth of a son shortly after 8 P.M., with the Conemaugh raging a few yards away from their back doorstep. Mr. and Mrs. Williams named their son Flood Charles Williams.

Mrs. Nettie Rhodes gave birth to a son while being carried on a mattress by six men. Up to their armpits in water, they struggled up a hillside until they reached a point well above the waters flooding Johnstown. Mrs. Rhodes and her newborn son were placed under a tree and came through the ordeal in good condition, although it was days before her husband, John, could find proper medical care for them both. The boy was named Flood S. Rhodes.

. . . Eight-year-old Gertrude Quinn, separated from her father, brother and sisters, was floating on a mattress with Maxwell McAchren. They were fortunate enough not to be in the main current of the flood, which would have dashed them down upon the jam at the Stone Bridge and thrown them in the grinding mass of debris. Drifting along on the fringe of the flood, they looked for an opportunity to transfer themselves to some more substantial refuge.

They floated toward a small white building jutting out of the water on a hillside. Here one of the more efficient rescue teams was in operation. It consisted of Henry Koch, the owner of a small hotel, and his Negro porter, George Skinner. Skinner held Koch out over the turbulent water by his knees—a perfect case of trust between employer and employe, if ever there was one—and Koch grabbed whoever came close enough to reach. Gertrude and her protector came close to the house but not close enough to be grappled in this fashion. There was nothing to do but throw Gertrude from the raft to the two men leaning out the attic window of the all-but-submerged hillside dwelling, a calculated risk, but better than drifting on downstream and facing the possibility of capsizing or being crushed to death.

"Throw that baby over to us," Koch called.

"Do you think you can catch her?" McAchren asked.

"We can try!"

So, Gertrude wrote later, "Maxwell McAchren threw me across the water. Some said twenty feet, others fifteen. I could never find out so I leave it to your imagination. It was considered a great feat in the town, I know." The main thing was, George Skinner caught the terrified and almost naked child. An overwrought newspaper account later compared her to "Little Eva" and Skinner, "the gallant colored fellow," to "Uncle Tom," and gushed, "George has a black skin, but his soul is white and his heart is in exactly the right place." Gertrude never felt this "hurried pen picture" quite did the heroic Skinner justice.

McAchren swam close enough to be hauled in by Koch. He saw to it that Gertrude was bundled in a dry blanket and watched her carried up the hill to a house where the women-folk could look after her. Gertrude and her rescuer never saw each other again, curiously enough, although both lived in the city for many years. Or perhaps not so curiously, when one considers the mutually exclusive social strata enjoyed by a workingman and the daughter of an upper-mid-dle-class mercantile family. Forty-odd years later Gertrude read McAchren's obituary notice in the Johnstown *Tribune* and sent a bouquet of dark red roses to his funeral.

A crowd of refugees was waiting on the hilltop and gathered around Gertrude when she was brought up there in Skinner's arms. She was not so numb with shock and exposure that she could not remember long afterward her resentment of their gaping, impersonal curiosity, their insistence that her face be uncovered so they could look at her. She particularly remembered one red-faced man with a tip-tilted nose whose stare was particularly offensive, and her rather irrelevant thought, "I'd like to pull his funny little nose for staring down at me."

Gertrude was taken to the home of a Mrs. Metz in a three-story wooden frame building which housed six families.

The Survivors Fight for Their Lives

Mrs. Metz had her own large family and a number of other guests to take care of but busied herself immediately with thawing out the child. Gertrude was encased in red flannels, which soon caused her to itch, and Mason jars filled with hot water helped to restore her circulation.

It was dark by now, and after being fed Gertrude was tucked into a cot in a bedroom upstairs. Occupying the bed were the "three Bowser girls," twittery spinster sisters who would still be known as "the girls" when they were withered old ladies. In the darkness, "a little yellow light from a nearby lamp shone like a diamond."

The Bowser sisters kept climbing out of bed and looking out the window at the ruins of Johnstown, exclaiming and gasping to each other over the awful spectacle. Though they whispered to each other to avoid disturbing the supposedly sleeping child, she could "pick out such words as 'frightful, terrible, ghastly.'"

Gertrude slipped out of her bedclothing and padded over to the window to see for herself. "There I beheld what was once our town, which was home and all we loved. I saw nothing but water, and two or three big fires reflecting over the waves, looking for all the world like ships burning at sea."

The sight forcibly impressed on the child the despair of her situation. She knew her home had been destroyed and that her aunt, cousin and nurse had lost their lives; her brother, Vincent, must have been caught downtown when the flood came; her father and sisters might have been overwhelmed before they reached the top of Green Hill with the flood lapping at their heels; she had no idea what could have happened to her grandparents, her aunt Barbara Foster and her family; only her mother was certainly safe. Gertrude

145

cried herself to sleep on the strangers' cot, with reflections from the fire dancing on the walls of the room.

Johnstown was, in every sense of the word, a dead city. Its population had been decimated.

All forms of communication with the outer world, telephone and telegraph, mail and rail, were blacked out.

The valley was swept clean of the Pennsylvania Railroad's main line to Pittsburgh, 20 miles of track to the east of Johnstown carried off like jackstraws, and the Baltimore & Ohio's trackage had been torn up for a mile stretch along the Stonycreek.

Six of Johnstown's 35 physicians had lost their lives, leaving a scattered and inadequate medical force to care for the hundreds of injured and sick and to cope with the possibility of epidemics—particularly typhoid and malaria—in the immediate backwash of the flood.

The police and other law-enforcement agencies were no longer functioning. The jail and its solitary prisoner were gone. The sheriff was last seen whirling down the Conemaugh on a piece of wreckage.

Except for those on the hills, most of the city's dwellings had been uprooted and were jammed together with those of the upriver boroughs and villages in the drift behind the Stone Bridge. Most of the people were homeless and had lost everything they owned, some of them literally stripped to the skin.

The gas and electric-light works had been destroyed and there was a continuing danger of explosion from the natural-gas mains, which might destroy what was left of the city.

Every factory, mill and shop from Mineral Point to Sheridan Station was either in ruins or covered with layers of water and silt.

Food and medical supplies, clothing and blankets, were swept away with everything else.

It was a dead city, cut off from the world by flooded rivers.

8. The Town Counts Its Dead

THE NEXT day, Saturday, June 1, dawned bright and clear. The rivers were perceptibly lower, the water in the streets of the drowned boroughs was sinking, and the fires in the churches and other buildings were burning themselves out. The worst, barring another storm, was apparently over. Or was it? Perhaps the worst was still to come, even under the cheerful June sunshine—the immense job of cleaning up, the agonizing scenes as families sorted themselves out and counted up their private casualty lists, the recovery and identification of the dead, the prevention and control of disease, the overwhelming task of rebuilding.

By now the outside world was well aware of Johnstown's plight. Downriver towns knew what had happened an hour or two after the city was destroyed, not merely from the masses of wreckage which escaped from the barricade of the Stone Bridge but more alarmingly from the number of animal and human bodies that were swept downstream. Telegraph operators on the all-but-submerged tower at Sang Hollow, four miles below Johnstown, were plucking people out of the river and hauling them onto their roof soon after the flood struck the city. At Bolivar, people on the flooded banks of the Conemaugh grappled for and removed 11

148

corpses, plus one small boy who had miraculously kept himself alive in the terrifying process of being dashed downstream. Two hundred and fifteen bodies were recovered at the river town of Ninevah, which became known as "The New Golgotha" in the newspapers. Other bodies were found to have been snagged in the branches of the chestnut trees lining the deep cut of the Packsaddle gorge where the Conemaugh emerged from the mountains, rose above the Pennsylvania Railroad tracks and swelled over the treetops for a short time. In Pittsburgh, too, on that corpse-ridden Saturday, watchers on the banks of the Allegheny began fishing out the flood's victims; towns on the Ohio and even the Mississippi were reporting that they had recovered bodies from Johnstown. Pittsburgh also was the scene of one of the more inexplicable miracles of the flood: a five-month-old baby was found on the floor of a wrecked house which had floated down from Johnstown. Quite alone, he had survived more than 18 hours on the flooded rivers without food or attention.

In Johnstown itself, the stunned survivors crept out of the ruins where they had sought shelter during the night, thanked God for the burst of sunlight, wondered for a moment whether it had all been a nightmare, and knew abruptly that it hadn't. George Gibbs of the *Tribune* graphically described their feelings:

Men who were the first to leave the wreck on which they had passed the weary hours were shouting everywhere. Rafts were out. Hearts beat again. Hope rose with the sun. The birds sang their most cheerful songs. A flag or two, still at half-mast as on Memorial Day, fluttered in the breeze, and we knew the country would hear our cry.

Then came the real awakening.

We must learn the truth the quickest and shortest way.

We must find our friends or their bodies. We must live. So out poured the saved. But soon they realized their helplessness. People went over miles of debris, at the risk of life and limb, to find no sign of their homes.

Where the houses had stood was bare ground, or perhaps the wreck of a house that the day before had stood miles away. The Cambria mills were wrecked—not hopelessly, but sadly wrecked. The Gautier and Woodvale mills were gone and so was every business house in town—or, if the building remained, the merchant moved among us, a tramp like the rest.

Freight cars, carried long distances, stood in the streets. At one place was a locomotive that had ridden on the bosom of the flood like a toy. Here was a big hotel, filled with people when the flood came, nothing left of it—even the cellar to be dug over again. Strong brick blocks mowed down like our colored farmer used to cut the grass in the park.

Hands of the dead stuck out of the ruins. Dead everywhere you went, their arms stretched above their heads almost without exception—the last instinct of expiring humanity grasping at a straw. Whole families swept away— here and there three generations. Whole families saved— the mockery of fate.

Where to go, what to do, no one could tell. The survivors were moving, but they knew not whither. Over and under the wrecks they went, in and out of the ruins—hoping, dreading to find a friend. The bridges were gone and the rivers divided us. In parts of the town there was still a waste of waters. Food there was none except up on the hills, and even there the prudent housewives had depended on the Saturday's marketing for their supplies, and their charitable hearts were sore because they could not feed the hungry. . . .

Warmed by the morning sun, the people's spirits were reviving. E. B. Entworth, an energetic young man who worked for the Cambria Iron Company, organized a flotilla of four boats to circle the drift behind the Stone Bridge and remove those who clung to whatever was out of reach of the fire. Entworth told reporters that he and his friends managed to take hundreds of survivors off the debris. None of them were more chipper than a young woman and her grandfather who had spent the night on the broken roof of their home.

The young woman had a broken arm. Under her other arm she carried a baby boy, who seemed to have inherited the family insouciance and was waving his arms and gurgling at his rescuers.

The young mother jumped nimbly into the boat and looked rather surprised when the men sprang to her assistance. "I'm all right," she said. "So's my baby . . . Wait, don't move off yet."

"Have you forgotten something?" Entworth inquired.

"Not exactly." She raised her voice lustily. "Hey, Grandpa," she called. "Come on, we're being rescued."

A white-haired old fellow, agile as a monkey, clambered over the rooftop and jumped into the boat. "Gentlemen," he said, courtly as a grand vizier, "can any of you give me a chew of tobacco?"

Most of the survivors, Reverend Beale related, were much less cheerful about their predicament. He and his family decided to leave Alma Hall that Saturday morning, having noted that "the waters had somewhat subsided, having forced a way through the wreckage under the arches of the bridge." The Beales walked five blocks over to Adam street through a shambles "filled with rubbish, such as cars, houses, bridges, trees and furniture, together with dead bodies," all of which were "piled up fifteen or twenty feet high."

Three thousand persons, they found, were gathered on

the hill at the foot of the Frankstown road. "Every one of that vast crowd was either injured in some form or had been bereft of kin or loved ones. Their agony was so intense as to be oppressive and held them in the grip of a vise, so that no one was seen to shed a tear. As fast as possible, the women and children were distributed in homes on the hills. These being few, and for the most part small, they were taxed to the utmost. In one dwelling thirteen families were located; in another nineteen persons slept on the floor of one of the rooms without a change of clothing." Reverend Beale and his family walked farther out along the quagmire of a road until they reached the home of friends on Singer Hill in Daisytown.

Cyrus Elder, general counsel of the Cambria Iron Company, was learning the fate of his wife and daughter, from whom he had been separated by a prong of the flood. Cut off from his own home, he had proceeded to his brother's house on Bedford street shortly before four o'clock the previous afternoon. When the flood roared around the lower floors of the house, he was struck on the head by falling timbers but his brother and sister-in-law managed to haul him upstairs to the third floor. The house withstood the nightlong battering.

Next morning, still groggy from his head injury, he set out for his own home with his brother at his side. They found the stately brick structure shattered and his wife and 23-year-old daughter Nannie missing. They were, in fact, never recovered, and finally were listed in the long roll titled "Not Known to Be Found," many of whom were buried anonymously in Grandview cemetery.

Elder was a practical man, and rather than uselessly agonizing over the presumed death of his wife and daughter, immersed himself in the work of reconstruction. There was plenty of that, with the Gautier works totally destroyed and the main Cambria mills, situated below the confluence of the Little Conemaugh and the Stonycreek, covered with five feet of silt under layers of slime and wreckage and water.

He established his headquarters in the First National Bank as soon as it was drained and adequately cleaned up. In the bank's vaults were $500,000 in cash and thousands more in other liquid assets; that included $125,000 for the Cambria Iron payroll, which was supposed to have been paid out that post-flood Saturday morning. Long after the flood the story persisted that a gang of opportunists descended on the bank the night of the flood, blew open the vault and made off with $10,000. Actually, if any little group with so much enterprise and a talent for safecracking had undertaken such an operation, they would have come away with half a million dollars rather than a paltry ten thousand.

The eldest son of Hetty Ogle, manager of the Western Union office, climbed over the wreckage on Main street to search for his mother and 19-year-old sister Minnie, who was her mother's assistant. Even from a distance he could see that the three-story building which had housed Western Union had not survived. But he refused to believe that the doughty Mrs. Ogle was not alive somewhere in the town. He remembered a few years back when she had a serious operation. His mother was so widely admired and cherished that the mill whistles were kept silent during the critical period just after the operation and bulletins were issued almost hourly to the townspeople. When he saw her shortly after the operation, she was too weak to speak to him but he saw that her fingers were tapping out a message in Morse Code on the covers. "It is over," his mother's fingers told him. "I am safe." Those fingers, he soon learned, would never tap out another message. The bodies of his mother and sister, along with those of the rest of the Western Union staff, were found in the ruins of the building. That night, over all the circuits of the Western Union, the message went out to punchers everywhere:

H. M. OGLE DIED IN THE JOHNSTOWN FLOOD.

J. L. Smith, the stonecutter who took his wife and three children to the Hulbert House for safekeeping, was frantically digging in the ruins of the hotel. He and a group of rescue workers found Mrs. Smith and her children in the rubble. It was a matter of tragic irony for Smith that, had he not insisted on their taking shelter at the hotel, they would have survived. Their own flimsy wooden house was left standing when the flood had passed. It was one of a row of such houses on Stonycreek street which survived, while stoutly built brick houses near by were destroyed.

The flood, George Gibbs of the *Tribune* observed, was most effective in leveling social distinctions, rigorous as they were in the world of 1889. Every able-bodied man pitched into the task of working through the wreckage for possible survivors, Gibbs noted. "Here a banker or merchant, by his side a laborer or perhaps a despised Hun. Here in the filth, all that was left of a sweet, refined woman; there and all about her the bodies of stranger dead. Here and there, wherever the wreckage landed, a fond mother with her dead babe clasped in the arms of death. . . ."

Frederick Krebs, his wife and her cousin came down from the attic of their home on Napoleon street. Almost every house in the neighborhood had been carried off its foundation, but the Krebs home was solidly built and stood six feet above the street level. Water was still standing up to the top step of the porch, but Krebs and his womenfolk were able to venture down to the first floor.

Eighteen inches of silt overlay the floor—but that wasn't the worst of the horrors that met their eyes.

The door leading from the porch had been ripped off its hinges and the body of a two-year-old boy protruded from the silt. Through the bay windows of the dining room they could see the body of a woman impaled on the picket fence surrounding the house.

They were glad to leave that house, for the time being, when a crew of volunteers from Kernville, the section of Johnstown located in the loop of the Stonycreek, poled their raft right up to the porch and took them aboard. Still aghast at the horrors visited upon their home, they were conveyed to the nearest high ground, Kernville Hill, where hundreds of other survivors were gathered. And the first sight that met their eyes there was the bodies of a family of eight laid out side by side along the Millcreek road.

In the sodden hills east of Johnstown the most bedraggled theatrical company in the world, at the moment, was struggling toward food, shelter and dry clothing, their Broadway finery wrinkled and soiled. The ladies of the company shook themselves like angry wet hens, cursing the day they had decided against domesticity in favor of the bright illusions of the theater; the actors, clinging to the baggage which contained their best suits and linen, stumbled over the wet uplands.

This, in all its misery, was the touring company of *Night Off*, a comedy sent on the road by the imperious producer-manager, Augustin Daly. On the night of May 30, the day before the flood, they had appeared at the Opera House in Johnstown following the Memorial Day speechmaking. Next morning they took the early train east for Altoona, but it was blocked by the landslide near the summit at Lilly. That evening they heard the news that Johnstown had been destroyed. Nobody was going to concern himself with a band of stranded actors in the midst of all that calamity. They decided to strike out on their own. In any case, they took a fervent mutual oath: even if they managed to reach Altoona, there would be no show tonight. No sirree, not for them, after what they'd gone through. But for all their proclamations on the hillside, they gave a performance that night in Altoona after making an unglamorous entrance into the city on a work train.

Victor Heiser spent the night in an attic in the lower part of Johnstown with a score of other refugees. "Dawn," he wrote later, "brought a transcendent sense of relief." Athletic enough, for all the hours he had spent at his books at his father's insistence, he leaped from the attic window to an adjoining roof, disdainful of the crevasse below, "just like stepping off a subway train to a platform," as he subsequently described it. He started searching for his parents, quite resigned to finding them dead, since the last glimpse he had of them was at the window of their home an instant before it was crushed by the flood. It was a search that occupied him for the next two weeks, with visits to the various temporary morgues every night. He finally identified his mother's body in a morgue, but his father's was never found. Friends of his family took charge of him the first few days on the farm where he had spent his allotted month each summer. Then he went to live with an uncle and aunt, Dr. and Mrs. Frank S. Schill, and worked as a plumber's assistant to earn the money for his education. All that was found of his family's possessions was a trunk containing some flat silver, his mother's Bible and his father's Civil War uniform with a penny in one of its pockets. He soon left the city and its memories, "ready for college but ill-prepared for life," and undoubtedly quite unaware of the great career in medicine that awaited his adult years.

Gertrude Quinn and her family, scattered over the town by the exigencies of the disaster, were counting up their losses. Physically, the damage was appalling; her parents', grandparents' and aunt's homes destroyed, the family dry-goods store demolished, everything they owned floating down the Conemaugh—or perhaps the Ohio by now.

Considering the size of the family, however, its loss of life was proportionately less than most Johnstown families. The only member to have been killed was Gertrude's 16-year-old brother, Vincent. It was apparent from his actions in the hour before the flood struck that in losing Vincent his family and the community were deprived of a very gallant young spirit. That afternoon he was helping his Uncle Louis move merchandise from the dry-goods store on Main street to a barn on higher ground. His uncle suggested that Vincent stay on the hillside as four o'clock approached and the water was still high. Vincent refused, saying, "The rivers haven't gone down much. There might be trouble at home. I must help save the little girls." The boy was hurrying home when the first wave of the flood overtook him at Main and Bedford streets; "a man in the third-story window," his sister Gertrude wrote, "saw his straw hat come to the surface, spin around, float away and disappear." Several days later the boy's body was found in the back yard of his grandfather's attorney, Jacob Zimmerman, on Bedford street.

Gertrude's grandparents narrowly escaped with their lives. They were separated when the flood bolted up their street, and her grandfather found a sanctuary on the roof of a general store. Her grandmother was found the next day by her son, Louis Geis, her unconscious form stretched out on floating wreckage. Her scalp was torn from her forehead to the nape of her neck, and required 32 sutures, but she soon recovered.

Her aunt, Mrs. Barbara Foster, and her husband and six children, came through without a scratch. Their house on Jackson street, next to St. John's Church, survived the battering of the floodwater, being partly protected by the bulwark of the church, but it caught fire from embers cast down on its roof by the blazing spire of the church later in the evening. By that time the water was subsiding and the Fosters were able to evacuate their home safely, proceeding to a vacant house they owned on the Bedford street hill.

It was her energetic Aunt Barbara who rounded up Gertrude and the rest of her family. Just after daybreak she started out for Green Hill, where she was quite certain that the Quinns would take refuge. On the way, to her amazement, she sighted the bedraggled form of her little niece, Gertrude, standing on the porch of the Metz home. Mrs. Foster told Gertrude to stay right there while she looked for the child's father and sisters. Mrs. Foster found James Quinn and his three other daughters in the yard of a house on Green Hill where they had spent the harrowing night.

Quinn, distraught with grief and anxiety, could not believe that Gertrude was still alive. It seemed impossible that she could have escaped the crumbling of their home, which he witnessed from Green Hill.

"If it's true that she's still alive," he said finally, "I'll never punish my little towhead again." He was thinking of the times he had spanked her for tomboyish exploits in the neighboring orchards.

The Town Counts Its Dead

A few minutes later Gertrude was reunited with her father and sisters.

Quinn should have been assured then that his little daughter's feminine instincts were strong, if latent. She was wearing mismated shoes, one too small and the other much too large for her, which had been culled from the Metzes' attic. "This wounded my pride and my distracted father had to carry me," she later recalled.

Pride was an expendable luxury, as Gertrude soon learned. She and her family, proud as they were of their position in the community, were forced to line up at soup kitchens with the worst deadbeats in town—another instance of the temporary leveling influence of the flood. And when she and her sisters, days later, boarded a train to join their mother in Scottdale, they were not at all embarrassed when their fellow passengers, probably assuming that they were orphans, took up a collection and presented it to the four small sisters.

There were others who received unexpected benefits as a result of the flood. Jacob J. Swank found a small house jammed into his back yard in the Kernville section, with hardly an inch to spare between it and his own house. For several years Swank made inquiries up and down the valley in an effort to locate its owner. Presumably the family which had occupied it was killed in the flood, and the house, almost without a scratch on its paint, was carried to the Kernville section with the other debris. Swank finally decided it was there to stay, renovated it and rented it out. The little four-room, two-story house still stands at the rear of 625 Napoleon street and is still earning income for the present owners.

It didn't pay to give up hope, even in the midst of the

flood's worst perils. A Grubbtown man was working on repairs to a house in Woodvale when that borough was flattened by the flood. Seated on its roof, he was borne downstream to Grubbtown and carried past his own home and his neighbors, watching from the upper windows. He called out instructions to the neighbors:

"Say good-bye to my wife for me ... Tell her not to spend too much money on the funeral. ..."

A few moments later the house came gently to rest less than a block from his home, and the man who had just said good-bye to the world was able to leap from one raft of wreckage to another and arrive home in time to cancel his funeral instructions before they could be transmitted to his wife.

The flood exhibited enough freakish benevolences to furnish its survivors with conversation pieces for a couple of generations.

There was a couple married just before the flood came, according to the story picked up by a New York *Sun* reporter. The whole wedding party ran up to the second floor, then the third, in the home of the bride's parents. They all stayed through the night in those cramped quarters. Shortly after daybreak the bride and groom, their parents and the wedding guests, emerged from the house in all their finery and picked their way over the wreckage, the ladies squealing in fear of soiling the hems of their gowns in the muddy water, so absorbed in this performance that they did not consider the possibility of sinking into the oozing wreckage and being trapped below. When they reached safety, the dangers they had just surmounted became apparent to them, and one lady promptly collapsed.

Some of the city's livestock had amazing and often inexplicable escapes. A mare standing in a downtown alley was engulfed by the flood. Several days later she was found in a stable a half mile away, muddy but unhurt. Rescue crews digging under two wrecked freight cars a few days after the flood found a stable buried under them. Inside, dry and snug, they found a cow chewing on her cud, a small dog barking at the cow, and five angry hens clucking at the dog.

The Victorian modesty of the women sometimes hampered rescue operations. Men working through the wrecked houses outside the rough triangle formed by the burning drift behind the Stone Bridge found women hiding in several of the attics, yelling for help and at the same time ordering the men to stay at a respectable distance. Realizing this was not an ordinary case of feminine perversity, the men finally had to deduce what the trouble was, the women refusing to discuss such a delicate matter with strange males.

The women had lost most of their clothing and were huddled in dark corners in their torn chemises and other unmentionables. They refused to be helped out but shrieked every time the men started to move on to more tractable victims of the flood. Finally, hunger triumphing over modesty, the women agreed to climb down on two conditions: the men would have coats or blankets waiting to cover their nakedness, and, on their word of honor, they would turn their backs while the women descended. The mission was finally accomplished in an agony of mutual embarrassment.

Even less apropos than ultra-modesty was a billboard standing just east of the Pennsylvania Railroad station. Untouched by the flood, it was plastered with a three-sheet advertising the Opera House appearance of the *Night Off* company then straggling through the hills to the east. Its red, white and black colors provided a garish contrast to the subsequent sight of coffins stacked at the depot and the waiting room temporarily converted into a morgue.

"INTENSELY FUNNY," the sign's tallest capitals proclaimed, until days later when someone tore down the inappropriate sentiment.

9. The Press Descends

THE EDITORS of the nation's daily newspapers quickly seized upon the Johnstown flood as the biggest news break since Appomattox. From all the larger eastern cities, reporters were sent hurrying toward Johnstown, accompanied by sketch artists, photographers and telegraph operators. Editors from as far away as San Francisco dispatched their star reporters.

By special train, by handcar, on horseback and on foot the reporters beat their way to Johnstown, racing to be the first to find out what really happened to the city, cut off in the first hours of its extremity from the rest of the world.

The editors naturally saw in the disaster a chance to boost their circulation figures. The Civil War had taught them that the public would read column after column of stories that gripped its imagination; not only the bare facts but the "human interest" angles. The flood had all the elements of a circulation-pulling story, with mass death and destruction, drama on every street corner, and the initial suspense over what had happened to the city.

Whatever the motives of their editors, the reporters who covered the story and gathered the raw material for all those circulation-winning displays in their home cities did a notable job of telling Johnstown's story to the world and attract-

163

ing the sympathy and aid which enabled the city to survive and rebuild. Their caste ideals, clannish pride and furious determination to get the story they were sent after were described, more than a little romantically, by Richard Harding Davis, the romantic hero of turn-of-the-century journalism, who was one of their number in covering the Johnstown flood. Part Galahad and part Nosy Parker, the reporter of those days regarded himself as a sort of foreign legionnaire with low pay, long hours, and bosses who delighted in cutting their staffs on Christmas Eve. It was a profession for the young and footloose. During the Civil War they had called themselves members of the "Bohemian Brigade," and bohemianism was still a totem of their craft.

Yet there was a certain purity of purpose about them—journalism was a high calling, although its practitioners were professional cynics—that evoked the admiration of so austere an observer as the Reverend C. N. Field, rector of St. Clement's Episcopal Church of Philadelphia, who had hurried to Johnstown as chaplain of the Guild of the Iron Cross. "If a few priests had been in Johnstown and had worked half as hard as these reporters, they might have done untold good. The reporters endured hardships of every kind—all for the sake of their papers and to give news to the world . . . I was ashamed of myself when I compared myself to a reporter."

The first word the press had of the destruction of Johnstown was a message sent the Pittsburgh *Commercial-Gazette* by Robert Pitcairn, superintendent of the Pennsylvania Railroad's Mountain Division, who reached Sang Hollow, just below Johnstown, about an hour after the flood occurred. He was on his way to inspect the damage caused by landslides east of the city which were holding up the Pennsylvania's crack eastbound expresses. When he saw bodies and debris plunging down the Conemaugh and listened to the stories told by crewmen on a work train which had been forced to turn back before reaching Johnstown, Pitcairn came to the conclusion that the city had been destroyed. He immediately wired the *Commercial-Gazette:*

> JOHNSTOWN ANNIHILATED. THOUSANDS OF LIVES LOST. URGE THAT MAYOR OF PITTSBURGH CALL MEETING AT ONCE TO ORGANIZE RELIEF MEASURES.

That telegram was received by the newspaper at 7 P.M. Two hours later it had arranged for a special train, with one car behind a locomotive and tender, to proceed as close to Johnstown as possible. That same evening the other Pittsburgh papers also chartered special trains and sent them racing to the scene of the disaster, including the *Dispatch, Post, Times, Leader* and *Chronicle-Telegraph.* But the *Commercial-Gazette* definitely had the jump on the story, thanks to Pitcairn, and its newsboys soon were bawling out the headlines:

EXTRA—A STUPENDOUS CALAMITY
The Conemaugh Valley Scraped Bare and the
Town of Johnstown Wiped Out by an
Overwhelming Deluge from a
Mountain Lake

Headlines on the front pages of other leading newspapers in their editions of Saturday morning, June 1, not much more than 12 hours after the flood, reflected the fragmentary and bewildering reports they had received from the small towns on the fringe of the disaster zone.

The New York *World* reported on June 1 with greater accuracy than its stories on succeeding days:

Johnstown

1,500 LIVES LOST
A BROKEN DAM SWEEPS
AWAY WHOLE TOWNS
JOHNSTOWN, PA., DESTROYED
HUNDREDS OF CORPSES FLOATING
DOWN THE CONEMAUGH

Next day the *World*, still without any word from its own reporters, jumped its estimate of the losses:

6,000 DEAD
JOHNSTOWN BLOTTED OUT
BY THE FLOOD
HALF ITS PEOPLE KILLED

On Monday, June 3, the editors again raised the ante:

THE VALLEY OF DEATH
HORRORS GROWING HOURLY AT THE
STRICKEN CITY OF JOHNSTOWN
10,000 PEOPLE ARE DEAD

And on Tuesday, June 4, the *World* editors added another 5,000 corpses, concluding that exactly half the city had been wiped out:

DEATH GROWS—A GIANT!
ONE PERVADING PRESENCE THROUGHOUT
THE CONEMAUGH VALLEY
FIFTEEN THOUSAND CORPSES

The New York *Times'* first account of the disaster on June 1 stated that it was caused by a waterspout, the nature of which phenomenon apparently was not perfectly understood

166

by the editors. A waterspout might wreck a small ship but never a city. The New York *Evening Post,* on the other hand, firmly announced that the true cause of the catastrophe was a break in the natural-gas mains and a consequent explosion.

Although closer geographically to the disaster that the newspaper editors were trying to describe for their readers on the basis of a few scattered bulletins, the Philadelphia *Times'* figures on casualties were just as unreliable as those of the New York newspapers. Its headline the morning of June 1 was conservative enough:

HUNDREDS DEAD

JOHNSTOWN OVERWHELMED BY A
TERRIBLY FATAL DISASTER

SUBMERGED BY A TORRENT

These were the dispatches on which its first account was based:

Beaver, Pa., June 1, 2 A.M.—Johnstown is entirely destroyed. Hundreds of lives are lost. The houses of the town were piled up in a jumbled mass and were being carried down the river before the flood. The mass of debris was afire and many people who were imprisoned were roasted alive.

Pittsburgh, May 31—Johnstown, the county seat of Cambria County, is tonight the scene of one of the most appalling disasters in American history.

Blairsville Intersection, June 1, 2 A.M.—A reliable courier just arrived states that 1,500 lives are lost in and around Johnstown.

167

Johnstown

By the time the edition of Sunday, June 2, came off the presses there had obviously been a conference between the managing editor and the circulation manager. Without any further information from the disaster area to support such a boost in the death toll—a fourfold increase over the night before—the Philadelphia *Times* reported:

DEATH'S VALLEY
HORRORS THAT SURPASS EVEN
THE WORST PREDICTIONS
6,000 REPORTED DEAD

While all this gaudy guesswork was being performed in the city rooms of newspapers all over the country, the corps of Johnstown-bound reporters was having a wild time trying to reach the city over flooded railroads. The Pittsburgh *Commercial-Gazette's* special train arrived in Bolivar shortly before midnight. The tracks were washed out, so the reporters hoofed it overland to New Florence, with one of their number hurrying ahead on horseback to secure the telegraph line. Reliable communications were going to be more valuable than any ephemeral "scoops" in the days to come. At 4 A.M. the first stories were being sent under a New Florence dateline, based on what the residents there had seen and heard. A refugee from Johnstown confirmed Superintendent Pitcairn's flash that the city had been "annihilated."

Actually, the first on-the-spot reporting of the disaster came from the Associated Press. Its general manager, William H. Smith, was a passenger on the Day Express, on his way back to New York from an inspection tour of the A.P.'s western bureaus. Standing on the hillside above the Pennsylvania tracks in East Conemaugh, he watched the flood

The Press Descends

roll over Johnstown—the biggest story of his career, right under his eyes. He stood there for an hour, fascinated and horrified by the spectacle, then remembered his professional obligations. No spry young legman could have done better. He hiked up into the mountains until he came across a road connecting several of the Cambria Iron Company's mines, flagged down an ore wagon, and persuaded—or bribed—the teamster to drive him into Ebensburg, 18 miles away. It was 11 P.M. when he arrived there. Only the Western Union wire to the east was open, so he started filing an account of all he had seen to the Philadelphia bureau. He wrote steadily for two hours, then broke off with a message that he was returning to the flooded city to take charge of coverage there. It took him until Sunday to travel the same distance, mostly on foot, that he had traversed in five hours on that fortuitous ore wagon.

By that time the Associated Press had the situation in Johnstown fairly well in hand. Aboard one of the specials out of Pittsburgh was Colonel William Connolly, a veteran newspaperman who served as the A.P.'s agent in western Pennsylvania. Accompanying him were Harry W. Orr, his best telegrapher, and Claude Wetmore, a freelancer ordered to the scene by the New York *World* as its correspondent pro-tem.

Their one-car train was halted frequently as trainmen walked ahead with lanterns to inspect the tracks for washouts. Finally, near Bolivar, the water came up to the driving rods of the locomotive and the engineer informed the newspapermen they would have to continue their journey on foot. Trudging along the flooded tracks, they fell in with a reporter from one of the Pittsburgh papers. It was close to midnight when they saw lanterns in the distance. A group of farmers had stationed themselves on a bridge over the

169

Johnstown

Conemaugh, equipped themselves with ropes, and were trying to lasso bodies out of the water without any conspicuous success. One of the farmers agreed to drive them over the mountains to Johnstown in his wagon. The fee was $50. Already people were scenting profit in the disaster.

Six hours later the newspapermen reached a point three miles from Johnstown on the south bank of the Conemaugh. It was 7 A.M. and a brilliant sun illuminated the horrors of the night before. Many bodies were sticking out of the muck along the riverbank. The Pittsburgh reporter became violently ill at the sight and decided to turn back, but Colonel Connolly, Orr and Wetmore pressed on. Connolly, for one, had seen a lot worse on the battlefields of the Civil War.

The three men slogged over the flooded roadbed leading into Johnstown. Connolly wrenched his ankle and the pain was so severe that he could barely hobble along. Orr and Wetmore helped him to a farmhouse on a nearby hillside. The ankle was so swollen it had obviously been sprained. For the time being, at least, Connolly was out of action. Orr and Wetmore agreed to handle the A.P. coverage between them. Wetmore was working for the *World*, but the *World* was an Associated Press client, so there was nothing unethical about the agreement on his side.

Just before reaching Johnstown, the surviving members of the party came across a lineman perched on one of the Pennsylvania Railroad's poles, just about to cut in on the line to Pittsburgh and transmit on his pocket Morse instrument.

"We're reporters," Wetmore told the lineman. "Could you send a message to Pittsburgh for us?"

The lineman was totally unimpressed. "Hell, no," he said.

The Press Descends

"This line is for railroad business only. You want me to lose my job?"

"All we ask is that you send a few words—let the world know that the press has arrived in Johnstown."

"I'll have to ask the superintendent if it's all right."

The lineman tapped out a query for his superior, and a few minutes later received permission to send a brief message for the press. Wetmore found a wad of soggy paper in one of his pockets and scribbled the few words permitted him. It was directed to the A.P. bureau in Pittsburgh with a request that the New York *World* be notified its special correspondent was on the scene. The message read:

OVER 2,000 DEAD. DEVASTATED JOHNSTOWN APPEALS TO THE NATION FOR FOOD AND SHELTER FOR OTHER THOUSANDS WHO ARE HOMELESS AND STARVING.

Those were the first of many millions of words to pour out of Johnstown to the nation's newspapers in the succeeding weeks.

Wetmore and Orr set up A.P. headquarters in an abandoned gristmill, and a few hours later Connolly, using a pair of farmers as crutches, came hobbling in to take charge. Orr and Wetmore ranged over the ruins, interviewed survivors, met the first relief trains arriving that afternoon from Pittsburgh and Somerset. Using the information they gathered, Connolly, despite the pain from his injured ankle, began writing a series of dispatches to be sent to the Pittsburgh office as soon as communications should be opened to the west. He used a board as his writing desk. Late that afternoon three wires were strung into Johnstown. One was reserved for the military, the militia having been summoned. Another was to be used for official messages, principally to the Capitol at Harrisburg. The third was captured by the

Associated Press, thanks to the durability and determination of its representatives on the scene. Western Union was reluctant to set aside one wire for a private organization, but Colonel Connolly exercised his most commanding manner to impress the telegraphers that A.P. represented most of the largest papers in the United States and was therefore something close to a public utility.

Telegrapher Orr, abandoning his reportorial duties for the moment, sat down on the key and began sending Connolly's dispatches. Within 24 hours of the disaster, the first newspapermen on the scene were describing it as best they could for millions of readers.

In New York, Boss Clarke, the celebrated night city editor of the *Sun*, deployed his forces with his usual superior generalship. The initial fragmentary bulletins convinced him that a disaster of the first magnitude had struck Johnstown. Clarke, one of the greatest city editors in newspaper history, had a certain affinity for flood stories. In 1874, he himself covered the famous Mill River disaster when the dam at the Ashfield reservoir broke and its waters roared down on Northampton, Massachusetts. Clarke attained a certain amount of celebrity among his fellow craftsmen for the story he wrote about a milkman who rode ahead of the flood and warned residents of the Mill River valley that the dam had broken. Oddly enough, he refused to give any credence to the subsequently disproved story that a similar rider had warned residents of the Little Conemaugh valley. Perhaps he had too intimate a knowledge of how legends are propagated to believe in any more heroic-rider stories.

Clarke was also celebrated for his deftness at plucking the heartstrings, and along Park Row the headline he wrote about the newsboy who was run down by a horse and wagon was regarded as an all-time classic. "A SPARROW FALLS," it read. The *Sun's* management could rest assured that Boss Clarke would not only cover the bare bones of the story but flesh it out with the "human interest" details which would grip the continuing interest of the readers. Shock would catch the reader, but it took reporting-in-depth to hold him, as Clarke well knew. He sent two of his best reporters, Daniel F. Kellogg and E. H. Chamberlain, to Johnstown, with more to follow on their heels.

The other New York papers also dispatched their best talent to Johnstown. The *Star* sent its Washington correspondent, George Welshons, since he was a little closer to the scene, and engaged a Pittsburgh reporter of imposing presence, title and name—Captain H. de Montreville, of the Pittsburgh *Times*—to represent the *Star* as its special correspondent. The New York *Times* sent William J. Kenny, its political writer and former city editor of the defunct New York *Press;* also Hugh Hastings, George DeF. Folsom and William J. Henderson. Among the New York *Herald* reporters at the scene were Alexander Kenealy, who was the son of a famous English barrister and Member of Parliament; John Tregaskis, R. H. Lyman and C. E. Russell. The *World* was represented by Richard A. Farrelly, W. O. Inglis, Hugh J. Beirne and George H. Dickinson. Walter Prentice was assigned by the New York *Journal*, not yet a Hearst publication, and Erwin Wardman by the *Tribune*.

One New Yorker had been covering a political banquet when he was summoned by his editor to join the platoon of reporters heading for Johnstown. There was no time for him to go home and change into something more suitable for the rough work ahead. After two days and nights spent on day coaches, wagons and buggies and on foot over muddy roads, he no longer looked like the perfect model of a gentleman journalist but more like one of those vaudeville tramps, his clawhammer coat in tatters, his boiled shirt spattered with mud and the soles flapping from his patent leather shoes. His colleagues raised an ironic cheer as he straggled into Johnstown. The New York *Sun's* reporters had to travel a thousand miles out of their way to make a connection, finally, for one of the stations below Johnstown. Rail facilities, heavily damaged by the rainstorms throughout the East, were already overburdened by people hurrying to Johnstown to find out what happened to relatives and friends. A group of Philadelphia newspapermen traveled to Harrisburg, learned that the line to Johnstown was still blocked by a landslide, and proceeded on to Cleveland, then to Pittsburgh and finally Johnstown, over various short-line railroads not yet overtaxed. The newspapermen from Baltimore, Washington and other southern cities were luckier, since they used the Baltimore & Ohio's relatively undamaged lines to Somerset and then up the branch line to a point on the Stonycreek about a mile from Johnstown.

Among the newsgathering professionals beating their way to Johnstown were a number of tramp telegraphers known as "gypsies of the key." These boomers, like vultures streaking for a battlefield, were infallible omens of a major disaster. Blacklisted from ordinary employment, the boomers were certain of being signed on for emergency duty during floods, fires and earthquakes. The reporters, none too straitlaced themselves, welcomed them as brothers in a nonexclusive fraternity. And with good reason: most of these veteran punchers were versatile and amiable enough to fill in for the reporters when weariness or too much booze overtook them. In some cases, the editors noticed a distinct improvement in the copy.

Among these birds of passage was a boomer known to his

fellows as "Old Bogy," the Casey Jones of his peripatetic breed, of whom an anonymous poet wrote:

> Few can wield a better quill,
> Shake a key with better skill,
> Crack a joke with keener jest,
> Store more beer beneath his vest;
> Yet with all his talents rare
> Bogy's tramping everywhere.

Newspaper editors in all the eastern cities were made aware of the intense public interest in the fate of Johnstown by the throngs which gathered in the streets outside their offices. Newspapers in those days plastered the fronts of their buildings with long paper streamers carrying the latest news in bulletin form. Thousands congregated outside the Pittsburgh newspaper buildings and stayed there Saturday and Sunday, night and day. Their temper grew violent when bulletins were pasted up reporting—with considerable exaggeration—that hundreds of ghouls were roaming the flooded ruins and robbing the dead. "Their indignation knew no bounds," one reporter observed. "They clenched fists and swore those who robbed the dead should not live." The *Commercial-Gazette* immediately began raising a fund to aid the first four trainloads of flood refugees to arrive in the city, starting the fund with its own subscription of $300. Gusky's department store used all its advertising space in the Pittsburgh papers to convey the management's sorrow over the disaster—and a nice sense of public relations.

In Philadelphia, too, staid as its journals generally were, the press described what was happening in Johnstown more by intuition than any information from its reporters, who had not yet reached the scene. The Philadelphia *Press'* headline ran halfway down Page One, beginning with:

Johnstown

A CITY OF THE DEAD
Johnstown the Scene of All the
Horrors of the Inferno
THE FLOOD'S AWFUL VICTORY!
Its Victims Buried in Trenches
Like Slain Soldiers
After a Battle
ROBBERS OF BODIES LYNCHED
Four Heartless Hungarians
Driven Headlong to Death
While Two Others Find
Speedy Justice at
End of Rope

Beneath it the lead story related that 30 undertakers and 11 carloads of coffins had started for Johnstown, and under a Ninevah dateline reported that "when the water receded from the fields over which it had flowed, there were exposed stiff, naked, bruised and mangled bodies of men, women and children lying in the mud."

Still cut off from firsthand accounts of what had happened to Johnstown, the newspapers demonstrated considerable ingenuity in giving the impression they had all the facts. They published considerable misinformation about the city, the region and its geography. Somehow the dateline Sang Hollow became "Smug Hollow" and "Songhollok." A Brooklyn newspaper reprinted a section of Charles Reade's novel, *Put Yourself in His Place* in which the bursting of a dam was described. That seemed like such a fine idea that a Cincinnati newspaper, a few days later, cannibalized the flood scene from George Eliot's novel *The Mill on the Floss*. Deprived of facts, the editors allowed their writers to wallow in the purplest of prose. Not the least gaudy lead paragraph was turned out by an earnest reporter for the Cincinnati *Times*:

> A pelion of calamity is piled with each passing hour here upon the ossa of calamity already showered upon this stricken city.

By Monday, June 3, seven Western Union lines had been opened to Pittsburgh—and the facts began to flow. The reporters on the scene clambered over ruins, coursed over the hillsides, visited nearby towns and villages where the survivors were temporarily quartered. Even at firsthand it seemed impossible to obtain a clear picture of the extent of the disaster. On June 4, four days after the dam broke, the New York *Times* declared that "fully 10,000 must have perished"; two days later, the New York *World* was still standing by that figure. It wasn't until a full ten days after the flood that most of the newspapers were close to the actual death toll of less than 2,500.

The working conditions of the newspapermen in Johnstown were extremely rigorous, and most of them fared much worse than the flood survivors. They had plenty of money but no place to buy food, and the leaders of various relief organizations refused to believe that a reporter could be as hungry and weary as a certified citizen of Johnstown. Most of the flood relief officials, in fact, were downright unfriendly to the press, although later it was conceded that the newspapers' portrayal of Johnstown's plight was "the spring which released the bountiful aid for the devastated town." In the first days of reporting the disaster, however, the correspondents operated under a definite cloud of suspicion and mistrust. "The Greensburg relief corps fed them on Sunday," a New York *World* reporter wrote. "Later Father Davis of St. Columba's helped them. Breakfast for the first few days consisted chiefly of cheese and crackers. They had to walk a half-mile from their headquarters to the railroad station for a cup of coffee."

The headquarters for most of the press was situated among the ruins of Haws' firebrick plant. They found shelter in a brick kiln left standing by the flood, used coffin lids and the bottoms of shovels for writing boards. Their telegraphic facilities were set up in a coal shed on the hillside above the Stone Bridge and its reek of death and corruption. Sam Kerr of the Pittsburgh *Leader* fell off the roof of a house while exploring an uncharred section of the drift and was injured so severely he had to be removed to Pittsburgh. Clarence M. Bix of the Pittsburgh *Post* fell through the gap in a railroad trestle and almost drowned in the waters below. The Pittsburghers organized the Lime-Kiln Club to commemorate their privations in covering the flood, and the New Yorkers formed the Flood Reporters Association, which in after years looked back upon the grim days in Johnstown through a haze of whisky, oratory and increasing sentimentality. The first meeting was addressed, one year after the day of the flood, by Adjutant General Hastings of Pennsylvania, who genially remarked:

"You stole my blankets, you lived on my ham, and you drank my whisky, but I feel, all the same, the deepest personal obligation to all the newspapermen for the way in which you stood by me in my efforts to mitigate the suffering of the people of Johnstown."

Whisky, it must be admitted, was regarded as necessary as pencil and paper to most of the reporters covering the disaster. One of the most talented whisky-hunters was Captain de Montreville of the Pittsburgh *Times*. With his ultra-military manner, he gave the impression that he was commandeering supplies in the name of the sovereign state of

The Press Descends

Pennsylvania. A colleague wrote that on one foraging expedition he knocked on the door of a drugstore in search of a "soothing lotion for the nerves." A woman's head appeared at a second-story window.

"Where in thunder is the druggist?" de Montreville roared.

"He's gone down the river," the woman said sadly.

"The devil he has! What did he do that for?"

"That's a question God alone can answer."

"Oh, that was it," the captain said, somewhat abashed. "Well, then," he conceded in a mumble, "he's excusable."

Along with the shortage of potables, the newspapermen were hampered by an influx of sightseers and other ghouls who descended on the city in an amazingly short time after the news of the disaster had spread. By Monday night, June 3, the thrill-seekers had already begun to arrive in search of their morbid delights. Many of them must have endured considerable hardship, slogging over flooded roads from the railheads.

The press subsequently found quarters in a two-story building near the office established by Western Union. They still had to use barrelheads as desks, and it was "drafty as a sieve and dusty as a country road," according to the New York *Times*. The reporters slept in a nearby hayloft to the "tuneful piping of hundreds of mice, the snorting of horses and cattle, the nocturnal dancing of dissipated rats and the solemn rattle of cow chains."

But it was food—after whisky—that became the primary problem. The *Times* men bought their first meal in the disaster area from a "pretty mountain woman with a delicious way of saying you-'uns." It consisted of gristly pork, bread and coffee. They were so grateful they gave the woman a dollar apiece. She promptly grasped the idea that there was money to be made in the midst of catastrophe and established a price scale that would have astounded the head-waiter at Delmonico's. Eventually, a *Times* man said, "It cost a dollar to go in and look around."

Obviously a more workable plan for feeding the press had to be found. The reporters hired a colored cook who prepared their meals over a natural-gas outlet at the brick kiln. But the reporters still had to scrounge around for the cook's provisions, and "every morning all hands were out bright and early sparring for food."

The *Times* reporter who described the working conditions of the press ended his account with a touching tribute to his fellow reporters (and himself, by inference): "Hungry, worn, footsore, disheartened, cold, lame and sick, they are telling the readers of their papers the details of the work here by that sheer pluck and indomitable energy which distinguish good newspapermen the world over."

The Associated Press seemed to be doing the most graphic job of describing the fate of the city. The story sent its clients on June 2, presumably written by Colonel Connolly, began quite simply, especially considering the fact it was an age when the rococo was admired in adjectives as well as in architecture. "Half the town seemed to be lifted from its foundations and swept away at once. The wreckage covered the water thicker than the houses stood in the town before. It was no longer a flood of water. It was a town afloat."

William H. Smith, the A.P. general manager, returned to Johnstown late Sunday to take charge of operations on the scene. Connolly worked 72 hours without food or sleep, despite the pain of his sprained ankle. A board resting on two barrels was his desk. Corpses and coffins surrounded him, part of the building having been taken over as a temporary morgue. On the night of Monday, June 3, he collapsed and Smith took him to Pittsburgh on a returning relief train. His successor was Alexander J. Jones, a frail man from the Chicago bureau, who cracked up after 24 hours without food or sleep. Meanwhile, Orr, the telegrapher, who had been alternating between legwork as a reporter and transmitting all that the other men wrote over the direct wire to Chicago, also caved in. Jones and Orr were also placed on a train for Pittsburgh.

Orr's replacement was one J. Herbert Smythe, of the Chicago office, a neat and precise young man whose habits more closely resembled those of a YMCA secretary than those of "Old Bogy" and other legendary telegraphers. Smythe was just as prissy as his name sounded. The other newspapermen predicted he wouldn't last the night.

But J. Herbert Smythe was no creampuff. He snapped on his armbands to keep his cuffs clean and sent out all the copy on hand. Then, A.P. still lacking a reporter in Johnstown, he tied string around the bottoms of his trousers to keep them out of the muck, and set forth to see what was to be seen. He wrote a 2,000-word story, transmitted it on the wire to Chicago, and meticulously sent along corrections as he checked over his copy. He lived on soda crackers and black coffee; kept himself neat as a ribbon clerk in all that mud and filth, and ran his competitors ragged.

A man named Lewis from the New York bureau arrived to reinforce Smythe. He had been attending a formal dinner in New York when he received the order to catch the first train for Johnstown. It took him three days and nights to travel the hundred-odd miles from Harrisburg by wagon and on foot. Lewis cut the tails off his dress suit and his collapsible silk hat was sadly battered when he walked the last few miles into Johnstown.

Other A.P. men arrived from Philadelphia, Pittsburgh and

Washington, and the Johnstown staff grew to the point where it became necessary to set up a separate headquarters in a gristmill. Food and water were in short supply for several weeks, and the only sleeping accommodations were coffins lined with straw.

To Smythe, however, there was something sacrilegious about sleeping in a coffin. He fastidiously made his bed on a board stretched across two kegs. However he affected his colleagues with his hoity-toity manners, Smythe turned in such a brilliant performance in Johnstown that the general manager—plain old Smith—breveted him a reporter in the field, and he subsequently had an outstanding career as an Associated Press reporter and editor.

A much more romantic type among the flood correspondents was Richard Harding Davis, then a rising star on the Philadelphia *Press*. The son of the managing editor of the *Public Ledger* and of a well-known lady novelist, he brought a certain distinction to the newspaper business—sartorially, especially—that aroused a great deal of resentment among the cruder types who believed a reporter must renounce anything that smacked of polite society.

Davis went to work as a cub reporter on the Philadelphia *Record*, whose city editor, Jim Chambers, was strongly in favor of the tobacco-chewing, whisky-drinking buckoes of the old school. Nothing affronted Chambers more than the spectacle of this unlicked cub strolling into the city room in full regalia, English-tailored lounge suit, long yellow ulster with green stripes, cane, and worst of all, kid gloves. Chambers claimed that Davis did not even remove those kid gloves to write a story. Yet nobody could call Davis a sissy. He was in the habit of covering meetings of Irish workingmen with a copy of the London *Athenæum* sticking out of his ulster pocket. One day Chambers' gorge rose for the last time. The city editor caught Davis lounging in the city room, just as though it were Philadelphia's most exclusive club, when he should have been out chasing a fire engine. Worst of all, he was reading, not the baseball results like any ordinary loafer, but an account of the cricket matches in England.

So Davis strolled over to the Philadelphia *Press* and got himself another job. He was out of the office when the first bulletins on the Johnstown flood came over the wires, and the *Press'* top reporter, F. Jennings Crute, was given the assignment. Davis moped for a few days until the city editor sent him to Johnstown to handle the human-interest angles of the story.

A photograph taken of Davis and other flood reporters showed him dapper as ever, with a pair of rubber boots as his only concession to the rigors of covering a disaster. The flood proved to be a long step up the journalistic ladder for Davis, whose stories were the only ones by-lined by the *Press.* He shrewdly allowed his colleagues to exert themselves on the more obvious angles and concentrated on the odd sights that caught his speculative, novelist's eye. He described for his readers the sensation of treading over thousands of cigars spilled from a ruined factory and providing the only solid footing in the neighborhood. He told of coming across a railroad car flung a half mile from the depot, with its admonition still visible: "Anyone injuring this car will be dealt with according to the law." He came upon the one-cell jail with the key still in the lock. Inside was the body of one John McKee, who had been arrested on a charge of drunkenness on Memorial Day, the day before the flood. He was due for release just before the flood came, having spent the customary 24-hours drying-out period. McKee had looped his coat over one of the cross-bars of the cell door and pulled himself up in an attempt to escape the swiftly rising waters.

Less than a year later the reputation Davis made in Johnstown carried him to New York and his years of glory as a war correspondent, a model for Charles Dana Gibson's square-jawed heroes, a novelist, and Byronic hero.

A few other reporters sought the significant detail, too, one of them describing the interior of a house whose occupants had fled or lost their lives. "The ceiling was gone, the windows were out and the cold rain blew in; the only thing left intact was one of those worsted mottoes that you always expect to find in the houses of working people. It still hung on the wall, and though much awry the glass and frame were unbroken. It was: 'There Is No Place Like Home.' "

Even as late as Thursday, June 6, six days after the flood, most newspapers were estimating the dead at four and five times the actual death toll. The Philadelphia *Press* that day announced in its blackest type:

12,000 TO 15,000 DEAD
The Latest Death Roll of the
Conemaugh Valley
JOHNSTOWN FULL OF COFFINS

Harper's Weekly sent two of its ablest staff members—W. A. Rogers, a sketch artist with a particularly graphic style, and Henry Loomis Nelson, a writer—on the heels of the first journalistic rush to Johnstown. They went to Philadelphia from New York but found it impossible to make connections for Johnstown; returned to New York and took the

The Press Descends

New York Central for Buffalo in the futile hope that they could make a connection there for Pittsburgh; continued west to Ashtabula, Ohio; caught a Pittsburgh & Erie Railroad train there for Pittsburgh, and finally engaged a special train from the Baltimore & Ohio to take them to Johnstown. Free of daily or hourly deadlines, unlike the rest of the correspondents, they were able to turn out some of the best reportage on the subject. Rogers' horrendous illustrations of families being swept into the drift, of mothers being torn from their children, are still being reprinted. Nelson wrote a calmly reasoned and dispassionate analysis of the causes of the flood, including these paragraphs:

"The story is as simple as it is sorrowful. It has been told in every awful and heroic detail and is now familiar in every household. If experience did not prove the probability of the situation, it would be incredible that great communities could live quietly in the immediate presence of an inconceivable possible disaster which yet could be readily averted, and take no steps to secure the common safety.

"But familiarity with such possibility often seems to paralyze apprehension . . . It is impossible that this event should not produce an effective determination that such disasters shall be rendered largely impossible hereafter . . . Its causes are perfectly comprehended; they are entirely avoidable; and a disaster of the same kind anywhere in any degree, after this appalling warning, would not only be a calamity but a disgrace."

The talent of Walt Whitman was pressed into service as the newspapers found ordinary journalese incapable of conveying the tragedy of Johnstown. The New York *World* spread his lamentations on "the waters that encompass us" all over Page One of its June 7 editions. It read in part:

Johnstown

Thou! Thou! the vital, universal giant force,
 resistless, sleepless, calm,
Holding humanity as in thy open hand, as
 some ephemeral toy,
How ill e'er to forget thee!

War, death, cataclysm like this, America,
Take deep to thy proud, prosperous heart.

The journalists, in fact, needed little or no encouragement
from Walt Whitman to soar off on poetic flights of their own.
One of the earlier dispatches from Johnstown in the New
York *Sun,* which must have escaped Boss Clarke's usually
discerning eye, began, "The time has not yet come to write
the story of the disaster that has turned the sparkling Conemaugh that rippled so pleasantly through the beautiful valley into a river of horror in a valley of death. Not all the
water that can flow from now to eternity can wash out the
color that has stained the bright mountain stream. . . ."

Threnodic prose such as the above inspired one of the
more celebrated anecdotes in American journalism. A New
York editor who sent an inexperienced but self-confident
reporter to Johnstown stood in the wire room and watched
his first dispatch come in, beginning:

GOD LOOKED DOWN FROM THE HILLS SURROUNDING JOHNS-
TOWN TODAY ON AN AWESOME SCENE OF DESTRUCTION . . .

"Break in there," the editor ordered the telegrapher receiving the story. "Send him this message."

The editor's message read:

FORGET FLOOD. INTERVIEW GOD.

10. The Scavengers Arrive

It MAY seem that with Johnstown
lying in water-soaked ruins, with death and disease everywhere, even the idly or morbidly curious would have had
the decency to stay away. But certain people are drawn by
the strongest instincts to the scene of every disaster. The
reality of other people's suffering fails to inhibit them from
pursuing their hobby, that of experiencing tragedy at sec-
ondhand. The scent of other people's grief only brings them
down in full cry, coursing over the ruins and scrabbling for
the humblest possessions of the victims. These gaping tourists, dull of mind and verging on the psychotic, quickly
invaded Johnstown.

The first dispatches from the city indicated that the foreign-born population was running wild, robbing corpses,
mutilating the dead, blowing safes, looting wrecked homes.
There were also lurid accounts of rioting, lynching, vigilante
action by enraged citizens. From the first sensational headlines it appeared that the flood's aftermath was more horrible than the flood itself.

Under the scarehead, "OMINOUS SILENCE IN THE
CONEMAUGH VALLEY," the New York *Times,* then
somewhat less chary of sensationalism, reported on June 3
that "tales of almost indescribable horror are coming to

light," that looters and rioters were running wild, and "the way of the transgressor is hard." The *Times* correspondent stated that 13 "Hungarians"—the miscreants were invariably "Hungarians" or "Italians," "Huns" or "Slavs," with the implication that native-born Americans just didn't behave that way—had been caught looting bodies at Sang Hollow. There must have been something bewitching about that name, Sang Hollow, because most of the atrocity stories came out of there, or were attributed to people living there. This account recited that enraged farmers pursued the ghouls and nine of them escaped but four were "literally driven to their deaths in the surging river." The report also declared that a "woman of genteel birth" had drowned in the Cambria Iron's clubhouse-hotel and her body was locked in a room to "prevent spoliation by wreckers who are flocking to the spot from all directions."

The same day the Philadelphia *Press* picked up the identical Sang Hollow atrocity story and reported it with embellishments overlooked by the *Times* man on the scene: "Every hour reveals some new and horrible story of suffering and outrage, and every succeeding hour brings news of swift and merited punishment meted out to the fiends who have dared to desecrate the stiff and mangled corpses in the city of the dead and torture the already half-crazed victims of the cruelest of modern catastrophes. Tales of almost indescribable horror come to light and deeds of the vilest nature are brought to light."

The *Press* reporter then related that farmers in the vicinity of Sang Hollow followed the 13 "Hungarians" also present in the *Times* version and saw them cut off the finger of a "dead and mangled woman." The *Press* agreed that nine escaped and four were driven into the river. It went further, however, and claimed that two other men were lynched by

The Scavengers Arrive

a posse near Sang Hollow after they were "caught in the act of cutting pieces from the ears and fingers" of two dead women. The posse, it reported, found the "bloody finger of an infant encircled by two tiny gold rings" in the pocket of one of the looters.

Quoted by many of the reporters as the authority for all these tales of loot-maddened foreigners was a special deputy named Chalmers L. Dick, a prominent lawyer and sportsman who was active in Johnstown politics. A leading Republican, he had served as burgess of Johnstown in 1888. The decidedly uncritical volume entitled, *Biographical and Portrait Cyclopedia of Cambria County,* published in Philadelphia in 1896 shortly after his death, commented on his activities in the days following the flood: "In the darkest hours . . . he was one of the first to take steps looking to relief, and to his unselfish work and indomitable will is due the beginning of what eventually brought order out of chaos."

Dick, who was the resident attorney for the Pennsylvania Railroad, was one of 50 deputies sworn in the day after the flood to preserve order and prevent looting until more formal arrangements were made. At best, if he was correctly quoted by the newspapermen to whom he seemed to be constantly available, he suffered from a rather bloodthirsty imagination. He told reporters that he was in charge of a posse and that "he had made up his mind to stand no more nonsense" from the foreign-born looters and "had given orders to his men to drown, shoot or hang any man caught stealing from the dead." Dick related that he and his posse had caught "seven Hungarians robbing dead bodies in Kernville and threw them all in the river and drowned them." Dick evidently made a firm impression on some of the correspondents, one of whom wrote:

189

Johnstown

Dick wears corduroy breeches, a large hat, a cartridge belt and is armed with a Winchester rifle. He is a crack shot and has taken charge of the deputies in the wrecked portion of the city. Yesterday afternoon he discovered two men and a woman cutting the fingers from a dead woman to get her rings. The Winchester rifle cracked twice in succession, and the right arm of each man dropped, helplessly shattered by a bullet. The woman was not harmed but she was so badly frightened that she will not rob corpses again. Some five robbers altogether were shot during the afternoon, and two of them were killed.

"Sixteen to 20" lynchings had taken place in the several days following the flood, according to this account.

The reporters asked Dick what he did with the bodies of the looters he shot.

He replied with all the nonchalance in the world, "Isn't the river handy?"

One of the reporters, evidently troubled by Dick's boasting, asked him, "Aren't the immigrants generally law-abiding?"

"I know better," he was quoted as replying, "for I saw them robbing the dead. Those I caught at it will never do the like again. Why, I saw them let go of their friends in the water to catch a bedstead with a mattress on it. That's the sort of law-abiding citizens they are!"

In this somewhat hysterical and definitely unhealthy atmosphere, vigilante groups sprang up, took potshots at almost anything that moved among the ruins, and concocted some of their own whopping fables about impromptu rendering of justice. At least one boasting account of their exploits reached print. "Quite an exciting scene took place in the borough of Johnstown last night," a New York *Sun* report read. "A Hungarian was discovered by two men in the act of blowing up the safe in the First National Bank Building with dynamite. A cry was raised, and in a few minutes a crowd had collected and the cry of 'Lynch him!' was raised. In less time than it takes to tell it, the man was strung up to a tree. Not content with this, the Vigilance Committee riddled the man's body full of bullets. He remained hanging on the tree for several hours, when some person cut him down and buried him with the other dead."

Other dispatches told of similarly drastic deeds performed in the name of preserving the law. Another special deputy was quoted as saying he had caught two Hungarians robbing the dead, chased them into the woods, fired twice and seriously wounded both men—an extraordinary piece of marksmanship. "From the latest reports," this account read, "the men are still living, but they are in a critical condition."

Such unofficial vigilance, it was written, "put a damper upon this soulless pilfering for a time."

The truth was, as subsequent investigation developed, "soulless pilfering" did occur in the first few days after the flood, but the tales of widespread looting, mutilations, rioting and lynching were all fabrications. Some resulted from overactive imaginations, some from the newspaper correspondents' reckless determination to pile the most violent melodrama on a story that needed no embellishment, and thereby outdo their rivals. The reporters who eagerly swallowed these fables were not required to check their facts or correct the impression they gave of Johnstown overrun by thieves and "fiends"; their editors felt no responsibility to retract the libels inflicted on the various national minorities. Nor did they stop to consider, in the first flush of these atrocity stories, that the "immigrants" were suffering a lot more than the residents living in their fine houses on the hillsides, and had all they could do to save themselves and their families without chopping off women's fingers to steal their wedding rings. No attempt was ever made to blow the safe of the First National Bank. A prosperous-looking corpse may not have been entirely safe from depredation, but Reverend Field, the Philadelphia chaplain of the Iron Cross Guild, told of finding the body of a businessman with $30,000 in cash intact on his person.

Reverend Field asked a militiaman patrolling the Johnstown streets about the truth of the rumors that the Hungarians were robbing the dead. "He looked at me knowingly, and answered, 'We call them all Hungarians when they do such things.'"

At least two newspapers, it should be noted, refused to give currency to such rumors. This was credited to the diligence of Alfred Reed, a member of the Pittsburgh *Commercial-Gazette's* staff and a correspondent for the New York *World*. The *Commercial-Gazette* editorially denounced the publication of such stories as "a shameful prostitution of the press," and the *World*, on June 4, published on Page One a cautionary dispatch from Reed: "No lynchings. I warned you yesterday not to print wild rumors, and am glad to hear you had enough confidence in me to hold out such stories."

After a long and careful inquiry, the Johnstown City Directory, published several years later, concluded, "Possibly there was one or two cases where a finger or ear was mutilated by a thief in robbing a body of rings and earrings; and one thief caught in the act was hung up to a tree till badly frightened, then told to leave, which he did in great haste. Another was thrown into the river but swam out and escaped; but had he been unable to swim he would not have been left to drown. Another was fired in the direction of, with a revolver, but not hit. This treatment frightened others, and it is likely very little robbery was committed by thieves."

Actually, the worst looting was committed by outsiders, the sightseers, the morbidly curious, the hunters of souvenirs and relics, who attached an incomprehensible value to the grisliest and most depressing sort of memento. A baby's shoe, a woman's locket containing a forlorn sprig of hair, any sort of family treasure, were all greatly prized.

For days after the flood, until the city was closed to rubberneck expeditions, the patched-up railroads into Johnstown carried almost as much tonnage in sightseers and opportunists of various kinds as it did in relief supplies and the materials needed for rebuilding the city. Among the incoming tourists were two men from Kansas City with criminal records; they and other suspicious characters were quickly rounded up and booted out of town by the tough metropolitan detectives from other cities. The two Kansas City crooks must have been only too glad to leave. That most ubiquitous of special officers, Chalmers Dick, rode up just as they were taken into custody and proposed that they be shot out of hand. After a bit of gun waving, Dick was persuaded to leave and the detectives escorted the visitors out of town. The special police wore tin stars of a nondescript design, easily copied, and a number of fly-by-night characters took to flashing them on startled citizens. This little game was ended when the constituted authorities collared every man wearing a tin star and demanded that he prove the right to wear it. It also resulted in the embarrassment of a number of earnest citizens who were quite proud of their tin stars and affronted at the necessity of proving they weren't impostors.

The first influx of visitors to the disaster scene were a raffish lot, according to a New York *Herald* reporter who rode on a train to Sang Hollow with a number of them. The man with whom he shared a seat was a drunken hunchback who was returning to Johnstown after years of absence, having quarreled with his parents. "One moment he was in maudlin tears and the next he was cracking some miserable joke about the disaster. He went about the car shaking dice with other inebriated passengers and won six dollars in half an hour. Over this he exhibited the glee of a maniac." Two dark-eyed passengers whom the others referred to as "sinister-looking Hungarians" aroused considerable suspicion. Swigging from their bottles, the other passengers loudly denounced "Hungarian looters" and worked themselves into such a state that it was moved and seconded that the pair be lynched on general principles. Just then the train pulled into Sang Hollow and the passengers tumbled out, their intended victims forgotten.

The newspaper stories also told of "alarming debauchery" among the visitors and survivors alike. "FIENDS IN HUMAN FORM," blared a New York *Herald* headline over a story which began, "The number of drunken men is remarkable. Whisky seems marvelously plentiful. Men are actually carrying it around in pails. Barrels of the stuff are constantly located among the drifts, and men are scrambling over each other and fighting like wild beasts in their mad search for it."

The thousands of workmen imported to help clean up the debris included a number who took their liquor where they found it. One group dug up a barrel of hard cider while working their way through the wreckage on Dibert street. By the time the barrel was emptied they were in the mood for a fight or a frolic, and chose the former. A free-for-all broke out and only the arrival of the militia halted it. A correspondent who witnessed the battle royal reflected that they did succeed in "demonstrating the proposition that hard cider will intoxicate."

The establishment of temporary jails soon discouraged such outbreaks. The old one-cell Johnstown jail had been carried off its foundation and deposited on Walnut street. After the body of its last pre-flood prisoner had been removed and the place cleaned out, it was made to serve as the municipal lockup again, and with a much brisker business. Most nights it was filled with caterwauling drunks. In East Conemaugh, lawbreakers were simply chained together and taken out under guard to work on the streets. The burgess of Cambria City also sentenced drunks and disturbers of the peace to be taken out under shotgun guard and placed on the work gangs without pay. The borough of Conemaugh built a new six-cell jail before undertaking any other municipal construction. Its first guest was one Patrick Maloney of Philadelphia, and thereafter the jail was known as "Maloney's Castle."

Not the least pestiferous of the visitors were the amateur photographers. It was long before the day of the handy little cameras which have become as much a part of the proper tourist's costume as his gaudy sports shirt, but the zealous photographer popped up everywhere with his box-like contraption, ungainly tripod, black hood and frightening blasts of flashlight powder. The New York *World* of June 8 reported that the amateur photographers were clambering all over the ruins and had finally exhausted the patience of the militia commander. General Hastings ordered a corral built, and all the photographers unattached to newspapers were rounded up and heaved into it with their equipment. Then they were taken out in work gangs and given a ten-minute workout with pick and shovel. Convinced by then that life is real and earnest and not merely a photographic subject, they were "ordered to get out of town and not come back."

Religious crackpots, who had to be handled more delicately, were drawn to the disaster scene and gave voice to apocalyptic visions. Some of them were inclined to draw a parallel between the destruction of Johnstown and the wrath visited upon Sodom and Gomorrah, a comparison which most survivors found irksome if not downright insulting. Few survivors, in fact, were able to take a kindly view of street-corner apostles who bellowed that a righteous God had ordained the city's destruction because of its sinful past —the city had its full quota of saloons and whorehouses, like any steel town—or hinted that death and destruction were exactly what the citizenry deserved.

The weirdest of the lot, by all odds, was a scraggy old goat who styled himself as "Lewis the Dominator" and "Lewis the Light," and proclaimed that the Johnstown flood had been decreed by him as a sign to humanity of his unearthly powers. Clad only in long red underwear, he invaded a Pittsburgh church on June 10, jumped into the pulpit and began his harangue. A flying wedge of deacons and ushers deposited him in the street. Lewis the Dominator was accustomed to such rough discourtesies. He next appeared on the streets of Johnstown passing out handbills proclaiming:

> Death is man's last and only enemy.
> Extinction of death is his only hope.
> Your soul, your brain ends by death.
> Whew! Whoop! We're all in the soup.
> Who's all right? Lewis the Light!

But it was the sightseers and souvenir-hunters who looked on a visit to Johnstown as a pleasant alternative to traipsing off to an amusement park, who caused the most trouble.

The Scavengers Arrive

Superintendent Meara of the Pittsburgh police commented that "there are too many visitors and not enough workers. There are more relievers than sufferers. A lot of dudes come down here and think more of filling their own stomachs than of relieving the poor." The excursionists, brought into town by the railroads until the authorities put a stop to this form of commercializing on Johnstown's tragedy, were not above standing in line at the soup kitchens and commissaries and saving whatever food they brought with them for the journey home.

On June 6, it was announced that no one could enter the disaster area without a pass signed by General Hastings of the militia or Sheriff Stineman of Cambria county. The New York *Times* exulted that "the curiosity boors are to go at last," and expressed itself bluntly on how the hordes of sightseers had "hampered, distressed and disgusted" those trying to bring the city back to life. One of the first actions taken by the city council of Johnstown when it reconvened for the first time following the flood was to request the passenger agents of the Pennsylvania and Baltimore & Ohio Railroads "not to get up excursion trains," explaining that "there has been a large influx of strangers and sightseers coming into our stricken community every day and greatly interfering with the work of clearing away the debris."

These measures were not entirely successful, and the curiosity-seekers still infiltrated the city.

The souvenir-hunters were especially resented by the city's survivors, who called them "respectable thieves." They did not scruple to pick through the ruins and carry off silverware, jewelry and heirlooms, as well as less valuable trinkets. They even invaded the ruined churches and stole hymn books, Bibles and vessels used in celebrating Holy Communion and other sacraments. Anything that wasn't

197

nailed down or too heavy to lift was regarded as subject to the right of salvage.

Not unexpectedly the natives found a way to take advantage of this craze for souvenirs. The townspeople installed themselves in "relic booths" and sold all sorts of junk to the simple-minded: horseshoes, corset stays, pieces of harness, pieces of iron pipe, buttons, even pieces of wood from wrecked houses. Late in June a dozen such booths were operating. A jeweler later made a tidy profit selling silver spoons with the South Fork dam represented on the handle, the waters rushing down the Conemaugh valley on the shaft, and the wreckage at the Stone Bridge on the scoop. It was an ingenious way of summing up the flood, perhaps, but no resident of Johnstown, remembering his dead, was likely to find it an aid to appetite or digestion.

11. The Waters Recede

AT THE moment that Johnstown was emerging from the ruins and looking around in horror and disbelief, much of central and western Pennsylvania was doing likewise on a smaller and less dramatic scale. Twenty of the state's 66 counties were seriously damaged by flood water on both slopes of the Alleghenies, as the Susquehanna and its tributaries, draining the eastern watershed, were flowing over their banks and swamping towns and farmlands. The West Branch of the Susquehanna had inundated the town of Clearfield, swept down to Lock Haven, at the confluence with Bald Eagle Creek, and carried a gigantic boom of logs downstream after submerging the town itself. At Williamsport it picked up another boom of saw logs, after flooding three-fourths of the city, and sent an estimated total of 150,000,000 feet of timber charging into the Potomac and finally into Chesapeake Bay. At Sunbury, where the West Branch and the North Branch join to form the Susquehanna, there was another flood situation, likewise downriver at Millheim and Coburn. Lewistown, Mifflin and other towns on the Juniata River were under water. The Susquehanna at Harrisburg, below its confluence with the Juniata, was racing along at 25 feet above its low-water mark and drowning the countryside, although the state capital itself was not seriously flooded. The Pennsylvania Railroad was badly crippled east of the Allegheny summits as well as below Lilly and down the Conemaugh. Along the Susquehanna, between Harrisburg and Renovo, six large bridges were carried off, and six others were wrecked along the Juniata between Susquehanna and the mountains.

Thus the cries for immediate help went up all over the western half of the state.

But it was Johnstown's muted first appeals that received the top priority. Lives had been lost and millions of dollars' worth of property destroyed in other sections, but Johnstown's hour of violence stood out so starkly that the world's attention was focused on it for many weeks. A few days later Seattle was almost destroyed by a catastrophic fire, but the newspapers could give it only a half a column of type. Even the accurate statistics of Johnstown's disaster were horrifying. More than 2,200 persons had lost their lives (between 2,205, the lowest official estimate, and 2,287, the highest). Three hundred and eleven children lost their fathers, 156 their mothers. Ninety-eight children lost both parents. One hundred and twenty-four women were widowed, and 198 men lost their wives. Ninety-nine families, with from two or ten members, were completely wiped out. To Pennsylvanians the battle of Gettysburg was a standard by which to measure disaster, and it was widely noted that Johnstown lost only 600 less than the death toll on the Union side in that battle.

Considering the lesser speed of communications in those days, the effort to relieve Johnstown of its more immediate suffering was organized with great alacrity. The Pennsylvania Railroad's capable division superintendent, Robert Pitcairn, alerted Pittsburgh to begin preparations to aid the city within a few hours after the flood had rolled over Johnstown. The Pittsburgh Citizens' Relief Committee was summoned to meet at the city hall less than 24 hours later, convening at 1 P.M. Saturday, June 1. It listened to a few speeches, and got down to business that afternoon. The committee paused only to hear the firsthand account of Johnstown's plight from Charles F. Jahn, a Pittsburgh businessman who had just escaped from the disaster area. "The people left there are struck dumb," he told the committee. "They can't imagine their losses. They can't realize what's happened to them. Hundreds are lying in the wet grass on the hills without food or shelter." Pledges of cash contributions were made at the rate of more than $1,000 an hour, a reporter noted. At 2 P.M. an emergency program was put into effect, with James B. Scott named as chairman. At 4:30 P.M. a special train pulled out of the Pittsburgh yards for Johnstown.

Aboard the 20-car train were 75 members of the committee, several doctors, 18 picked police officers, all crowded into one car. Another car was packed with coffins. The rest of the train was loaded with food, clothing, lumber and other supplies.

Normally a train would take about two and a half hours to reach Johnstown, which was 78 miles to the east, but it was 10 P.M. before the special arrived at Sang Hollow, making its way over flooded tracks and stalled frequently by heavy freight traffic which had been held up by high water and washouts all along the line.

The signal tower at Sang Hollow advised Scott and his aides that the train would have to halt there. A 400-foot section of track around the long bend in the Conemaugh up ahead had been washed out. That didn't stop the Pittsburghers. They hauled their tons of supplies on their backs over the washed-out trackage; fashioned a sort of platform car out of two handcars and some of their lumber; used this conveyance to carry their supplies up the wobbly track to where a work train met them and proceeded to the outskirts of Johnstown. Along the way they established supply depots at Cambria City and Morrellville.

By dawn of the 2nd Pittsburgh's first contributions to the relief of Johnstown were being distributed.

Actually, the first supplies to reach Johnstown came from the farms, mining towns and crossroads settlements in the mountains surrounding the city. This spontaneous form of help arrived within 12 hours after the city was devastated. People from the Frankstown Hill neighborhood, Whiskey Springs, Brownstown, Prospect and Morrellville simply loaded up their wagons with all the food and clothing and blankets they could spare and headed for Johnstown. A few hours later wagon trains toiled down the mountains from Altoona and Ebensburg.

On Sunday, June 2, the first two of a network of commissaries were established to distribute whatever supplies came into the city. On the north side of the Conemaugh, the needs of 10,000 residents were supplied by the commissary set up in the Pennsylvania Railroad station in Millville; on the south side of the river, other thousands were supplied from a commissary established in a vacant building at Vine and Bedford streets. Ten days later these were designated the main supply depots and 14 district commissaries were established up and down the valley.

The horror of the pile-up behind the Stone Bridge, the suffering of those who survived and stared down on the remnants of the city from the hilltops, and the immensity of the task of feeding and sheltering close to 30,000 persons, were so overwhelming that those coming from the outside were stunned. It took them a few hours to accustom themselves to the tragedy surrounding them. Not a few were so sickened that they fled without turning a hand to help. Most of the "relievers," however, steeled themselves to the long hard job ahead, a strong sense of compassion overcoming their repugnance for the gruesome sights and sounds that confronted them wherever they turned. They quickly learned that a certain healthy callousness was necessary. There is nothing clean about a flood; it had covered the city with a lake of filthy water and smashed a thousand buildings into the hillocks of debris behind the Stone Bridge. Corpses already were festering there, and slime and silt covered everything. Typhoid was flaring up. Worst of all, perhaps, was the fact that the debris was still burning. On the Monday following the flood, fire engines from Pittsburgh and Philadelphia had arrived to prevent the fire from spreading, and gradually extinguished it. "In the immensity of the disaster," one reporter observed, "their feeble efforts seem like those of boys with squirt guns dampening a bonfire." To Reverend Field, coming from the serenity of his Philadelphia rectory, there was a touch of the Grand Guignol, particularly the emergence of several persons who had survived five terrible days trapped in the ruins. This was the scene as he described it:

Trees and telegraph poles, houses and furniture, bedding and clothing, wire and bodies of men had all been burned and bound up together. The fire did not cease until it reached the water's edge, and now there was no trace of water in sight . . . As we passed over the bridge it was lined with men looking down into the dark, blackened mass below, where a few men were searching for bodies in the deep holes beneath the arches. Now and then a body would be detached and brought to the surface, and on this Wednesday after the flood the bodies of two women and an old man were discovered to be still alive.

The old man lived just long enough to give his name, and then fell back dead. A little child was found in another part on this same day. She had crawled out from the ruins, and was sitting on the riverbank playing with her feet. When she was spoken to, she looked with a blank stare and walked a few steps, but then fell in a state of unconsciousness. After some care, however, she revived, and the man who found her claimed her for his own. The poor man had lost his own children and found some comfort in caring for this little one.

Above the drifts, a New York *Sun* reporter wrote,

It is as clean of debris and wreckage as though there had never been a building on it. In reality it was the central part of Johnstown. Buildings covered it thickly. Its streets were paved, and its sidewalks were of substantial stone. It had street car lines, gas and electric lights. Iron bridges spanned the streams. Not a brick remains, not a stone nor a stick of timber. There are not even hummocks to show where wreckage might be covered with a layer of mud. Not even the lines of streets can be remotely traced.

A determined-looking little woman wearing a pair of muddy boots and a sort of field uniform, also showing signs of rough service, appeared at the headquarters of Adjutant General D. H. Hastings of the Pennsylvania militia on June 5. General Hastings was soon to have a full regiment, more than 600 troops, under his command to assist the local authorities in maintaining order, but he never attained the authority wielded by his elderly civilian visitor.

The general admitted to himself that his visitor, odd-looking though she was, gave the impression that she was accustomed to giving orders. She wore the habit of command as confidently as any three-star general. And well she might, for she had been taking charge of desperate situations for the past quarter of a century. She announced herself crisply:

"Clara Barton, of the American Red Cross."

Miss Barton, the "angel of the Civil War battlefields," one of the founders and first president of the American Red Cross, was then 68 years old. She had retained the vigor of her youth. Within 48 hours of hearing word of the flood, she had organized the advance echelon of Red Cross relief to Johnstown and set out for the city. Three days later, traveling over disorganized railroads and making her way on foot the last few miles, she arrived and presented herself to General Hastings.

The general hardly knew just what to say to the little woman who exuded confidence and self-assurance. He could hardly extend a formal welcome to someone who obviously felt quite at home in the midst of catastrophe. Miss Barton noted his confusion and later wrote, "I could not have puzzled General Hastings more if I had addressed him in Chinese; and if ours had been truly an Oriental mission, the gallant soldier could not have been more courteous and kind."

Perhaps the "gallant soldier" had a presentiment of the fact that he would soon be presenting himself at her headquarters instead of vice versa, and would himself be the supplicant. It was just as well that he immediately pledged Miss Barton any assistance she might require in setting up her advance headquarters. A week later, hat in hand, he was begging lumber from her to erect quarters suitable for a visit from the Governor of Pennsylvania.

Johnstown

Miss Barton set up her first tent and planted the Red Cross flag on Prospect Hill. Eventually her unit was increased to 50 persons, but those accompanying her to Johnstown numbered only five, including Dr. Clara Alexander, a native of Johnstown. Working at the dry-goods box which served as her desk, Miss Barton distributed almost half a million dollars' worth of money and materials, taking time out only for meals and a minimum of sleep. Her task was complicated by the clogged communications, with messages delayed 24 hours on the Western Union wires out of town, but soon money and supplies of all kinds were pouring in from every part of the nation and many countries of the world. About 25,000 persons received some form of aid from the Red Cross before the emergency was over. They came to Miss Barton and her helpers with only the clothes on their backs—in some cases not even that.

Most of the emergency medical work at the scene was performed by the Red Cross' Philadelphia unit, which had built up a highly efficient disaster service and came equipped with all the medical and surgical supplies needed for the moment. It set up a tent hospital at Wood and Cedar streets, with Dr. Pancoast in charge. The able young man who performed most of the emergency operations was Dr. John Richard Taylor, only a few years out of the University of Pennsylvania's medical school. The young surgeon was a member of a distinguished family; his grandfather was General Zachary Taylor, hero of the Mexican War and briefly President of the United States, and his father was General Richard Taylor, one of the Confederacy's abler and more literate commanders. Dr. Taylor himself, choosing to live and practice in the North, was an unself-conscious symbol of the slowly healing wounds of the Civil War. In the first days following the Philadelphia unit's arrival, he demonstrated his skill night and day under the cluster of lamps in the surgical tent.

A sort of rivalry sprang up between the Philadelphia unit and the Red Cross headquarters under Clara Barton. The Philadelphians, with their large and self-contained unit, sometimes felt that they constituted the tail that wagged the dog. The rivalry was all to the good as far as the survivors of the flood were concerned. The hotter the competition between the two, the more help they received.

Miss Barton, in fact, had all she could do to distribute the mountains of supplies that began arriving from all quarters. As a sampling of the sources of the donations: mattresses and bedding in large quantities were forwarded from the people of New Bedford, Massachusetts, and from the New York *Mail,* to be dispensed by the Red Cross; furniture and enamelware came from Sheboygan, Wisconsin; lumber by the carload was shipped from Illinois, Iowa and the Pacific Northwest to rebuild the city's homes. The campaign to collect food for the sufferers in Johnstown reached into every schoolroom in the land. Miss Georgianna Gray of Burlingame, California, recalls the day her teacher informed the class that Johnstown had just been destroyed by a flood and told her pupils, "You cannot do much, being so little and so far away. But you can help. Those people are hungry, and tomorrow morning I want everyone of you to come to school with a potato." Day after day, Miss Gray and her fellow pupils marched to school with potatoes and deposited them in a bin in the cloakroom, and "in my mind's eye I could see locomotive after locomotive hauling potatoes from Oakland, California, to Johnstown, Pennsylvania, and every potato must surely have been indelibly inscribed with the love and sincerity that prompted this very simple act of charity."

Johnstown

Housing was the most serious problem, once the people had been provided food, clothing and medical attention. Miss Barton supervised the construction of a large warehouse and three "Red Cross Hotels" from the carloads of lumber sent from the Middle West. The first "hotel" was built on Locust street on the former site of St. Mark's Episcopal Church. It was a two-story frame structure with 34 bedrooms on the second floor, a dining hall, sitting room and laundry on the first. Miss Barton ordered that the price of meals be kept to 25 cents each, or less. She was assisted in managing the hostels by Mr. and Mrs. John Tittle, a Johnstown couple who had narrowly survived the disaster themselves. They were caught on the roof of their home when it was carried off its foundation, one on each side of the roof and their hands clasping over the ridgepole. Tittle managed to hang onto his wife until the house finally was lodged against a bridge in Kernville. The Tittles were surprised to find that other members of the household had survived. In the attic, half drowned but still alive, were their Negro woman servant, their setter Rob and their parrot, squawking feebly in its cage.

There was a great rush for accommodations at the Locust street establishment, and it seemed likely that considerable bad feeling would be aroused among those rejected as tenants. Miss Barton reserved the right to select the Red Cross' guests, unable to resist dramatizing the announcement of her selections. She gave a formal tea to celebrate the opening on July 27. Some of her guests found keys beside their plates. That was notification they had been chosen as occupants of the new quarters. Somehow Miss Barton managed to charm those who had been rejected out of the sulks, and not a teacup was broken in anger.

The second "Red Cross Hotel" was built on Somerset

street next to the relatively undamaged Church of the Brethren, and the third, consisting of four buildings formed in a square and accommodating 16 families, in Woodvale.

That wasn't quite the end of her career as a builder. Toward the end of her five-month stay in the city, she bought six prefabricated houses, which were even then being developed, and grouped them into a Red Cross infirmary on Walnut street. Even so, the energetic and well-heeled Philadelphia unit outdid her in the construction of hospital facilities. The Philadelphians temporarily took over the management of the Cambria Iron Company's hospital on Prospect Hill, then set up a contagious-disease hospital in Johnstown and a dispensary in Hornerstown. Before leaving, the Philadelphia unit also organized what is now known as the Conemaugh Valley Memorial Hospital.

By the end of October Clara Barton was able to report that, "Enterprising, industrious and hopeful, the new Johnstown, phoenix-like, rose from its ruins, more beautiful than the old." Schools, churches, stores and factories were running again, and there was no further need of the woman who had chosen always to live on the knife-edge of a human crisis. The day she left Johnstown, she was presented with a gold pin and a locket, set with diamonds and amethysts.

Clara Barton was then at the height of her fame. In Washington, on her return, a banquet was given for her at Willard's Hotel. The guest of honor was almost concealed behind a bouquet sent by President and Mrs. Harrison. Miss Barton was puzzling to herself, she later told friends, over what to do with all the lumber that had been used for temporary construction in Johnstown, once the buildings were replaced by permanent structures. She felt that such material was given to her in trust and must be put to practical use. She finally worked out her problem. The timber used in helping to shelter the people of Johnstown was eventually used in constructing the rambling building at Glen Echo, Maryland, which housed the national headquarters of the Red Cross for many years.

Prodigious as were Clara Barton's efforts, they formed only a small part of the world-wide campaign through which $3,000,000 was raised and Johnstown was restored to well-being. The contributions to Johnstown's relief came in all forms and sizes. In Omaha, the postmen raised $50 and forwarded it to the ten letter-carriers of Johnstown. The Connecticut legislature appropriated $25,000 for Johnstown's relief. The New York *Mail* collected $49,000. Various lodges and fraternal organizations contributed a total of $260,000. Cincinnati sent 20,000 hams, almost one for each survivor. In Philadelphia, the police department's paddy wagons joined with vans, express wagons and carts in going from street to street gathering contributions, which came to more than $150,000. Many towns in Ireland sent money, and many of their people wrote letters of encouragement to the survivors. Subscriptions were opened by the United States consulates in London, Paris and Dresden. Many of the leading American prize fighters appeared at a benefit program at Madison Square Garden in New York, the feature of which was a sparring match between Charlie Mitchell and Jake Kilrain, who was to meet John L. Sullivan for the heavyweight championship of the world July 8 in New Orleans. The promoters said they raised "between $1,500 and $2,000."

The theatrical world, as usual, outdid everyone else in the spontaneity and generosity of its efforts to help the sufferers. On the Monday after the flood, Augustin Daly's road company gave a benefit in Altoona. Daly's own company, playing in *Lottery of Love* in Chicago, switched over to a matinee benefit production of *Night Off*, the last theatrical performance in Johnstown before the flood, and raised $1,200 that afternoon. Francis Wilson and his company raised $930 at a performance of *The Colah* on Broadway. Edwin Booth, the foremost actor in America, appeared in the third act of *Othello* at the Metropolitan Opera House and gathered in $2,500 for Johnstown relief. John Philip Sousa and Buffalo Bill gave benefits in their somewhat diverse fields.

The poor man's mite and the princely bag of coins all clinked into the various relief committee coffers. The Colored Baptist Church of Cedar Creek, Georgia, forwarded 55 cents, and the Sultan of Turkey contributed the sum of $876.57. Two years later the news penetrated Payne, Alabama, where a church raised $2.50 in 1891. Tammany Hall exhibited its customary vigor in raising funds; each assembly district was ordered to send in $100 and be quick about it, causing a momentary flurry among ward heelers, police captains, saloonkeepers, and other interested parties. A silver brick was sent to the New York Produce Exchange by the Board of Trade of Cupola, Colorado, with instructions to sell it and turn over the proceeds to a relief fund. A Confederate veteran sent $400 to the New York Stock Exchange in Confederate currency. He instructed that the bills be sold and the proceeds given the Johnstown survivors. No one ever found out whether this gesture was consciously ironic. From Victoria, Queen of Great Britain and Empress of India, came condolences only, but the people of England made up for her oversight or parsimony with contributions of cash.

The bulk of the cash contributions, however, was collected by the flood relief committees of Pittsburgh, Philadelphia and New York, each raising more than half a million dollars.

All over the country freight cars were moving toward Johnstown, chalked with such signs as "This car on time. Going to Johnstown. Must not be delayed"; "Stations along route fill this car with supplies for Johnstown"; "Braddock's Relief for Johnstown." Not all of these cars were carrying the most useful items. One observer noted that "many forgot they were not shipping clothing to a community of tramps."

To administer the more than $3,000,000 in funds raised by Pennsylvania's Governor Beaver, the relief committees of Philadelphia, New York and Pittsburgh, and coming in from other sources, a Flood Commission was appointed by the governor and included James B. Scott, Reuben Miller, and S. S. Marvin, of Pittsburgh; E. H. Fitler, Thomas Dolan, John Y. Huber, Robert C. Ogden, and Francis B. Reeves, of Philadelphia, and Judge H. H. Cummin, of Williamsport. Members of the New York committee included the city's most distinguished citizens, including Theodore Roosevelt, Daniel Frohman, Chauncey Depew, Grover Cleveland, Charles A. Dana, August Belmont and Jacob Ruppert.

The towns of western Pennsylvania provided assistance on a more immediate and homely scale. Brownstown's 53 families somehow provided living quarters for 1,500 flood refugees for two days following the disaster, and the people of Morrellville took in another 1,500. The courthouse bell summoned the townspeople of Indiana, Pennsylvania, to contribute whatever they could. Greensburg sent a wagonload of coffins, and the people of Latrobe dispatched $700 in cash and two wagons of provisions. Churches, courthouses and borough halls throughout the region were collection points for whatever could be spared by the people of western Pennsylvania from their own homes.

The Waters Recede

And there were many who contributed their services to the task of cleaning up and rebuilding the ruined city. The need for their personal help, their muscle as well as their money, was emphasized by a member of the Pittsburgh Relief Committee member whose description of this work was widely circulated:

> The anxious people crowded around the cars begging for something to carry to their homeless families. It was only after forming a line from the train to the temporary storehouses that the supplies could be unloaded and taken to a place where a proper distribution could be made . . . Within a few hours after the arrival of the train the yellow ribbon [which was the badge adopted by the relief corps] was seen in all parts of the devastated valley. Every man had come to work and help the afflicted . . . This was no place for rest or comfort, and it may be truthfully said that for forty-eight hours after arrival many of the relief corps suffered as much from hunger and loss of sleep as any of the residents of the valley.

The ignoble elements in human nature, unpurified by tragedy, continually amazed the relief workers. Most of the people they helped, of course, took no more than they needed for their daily meals, and were humbly grateful for it. But there were disillusioning instances of greed and arrogance. Before the commissary system had been organized throughout the valley, some of the surviving grocers were found marking up their prices to a level only the desperately hungry would pay, if they had the money. The grocers were dissuaded from further profiteering by members of the temporary government, who pointed out that a lynch rope might cut short their enjoyment of the proceeds.

At one supply depot a "pert" young woman, observed by J. J. McLaurin of the Harrisburg *Telegram,* shoved and elbowed her way through the crowd and announced in a loud firm voice that she would require instantly "two dresses, two sets of underwear, two pairs of shoes and two hats.

"*New* goods only," she crisply added.

The official at the counter said, "I am afraid you've made a mistake, young lady. This is a charitable venture, not a young ladies' outfitting establishment. Of course, if you could wait until tomorrow, we're expecting a consignment of diamond rings and gold watches."

The young woman flounced away in a rage.

A woman waiting in line said, "Why, that's Mary —— She's going to be married next Monday. She's gathering her trousseau together!"

Another client who took the relief measures for granted pawed over the dresses offered at a supply depot counter as impatiently as any shopper in a department store bargain sale. Finally, in exasperation, she turned to a relief official and said, "I lost a dress that cost twenty dollars. Fifteen dollars for the cloth, five for the sewing woman. I'm entitled to a twenty-dollar dress!"

A member of the Altoona Relief Committee noticed that one man seemed to be lining up for food practically around the clock. An investigation developed the fact that he had stored 15 sacks of flour and five hams in his undamaged home. His mumbled explanation was that "They're giving all this stuff away, and I thought I might as well get my share."

The New York *Herald* charged that food distribution was often so haphazard that the flour and ham collector was almost justified in his views. As an example of the "mismanagement" it alleged, the *Herald* described the scene when cars loaded with supplies arrived from Beaver Falls. Relief workers tossed bread, sacks of coffee and cans of meat "as they would unload bricks, throwing them out without look-ing where they went." One woman had six packages of coffee, and nothing else, wrapped in her apron. Several small boys were grabbing all the supplies they could and hiding them "under a switch target," the *Herald* reporter observed, and "actual sufferers got little or nothing . . . It was like throwing a handful of pennies into a mob of Italian beggars."

Most such abuses were soon corrected, however, as relief officials gained experience and learned that the victims of a disaster may be pathetic in the mass but individually re-tain the failings they had before misfortune overtook them. . . .

In the matter of organizing a temporary government, the responsible citizens of Johnstown had moved swiftly and efficiently. On Saturday afternoon, June 1, the day after the flood, they met at the Adams street schoolhouse and formed a committee to govern all the affairs of the devastated city. Other boroughs made similar arrangements. They had to start from scratch, with many former officials of the city gov-ernment dead, missing or incapacitated. In the borough of Johnstown, for instance, the burgess was missing; the chief of police had lost his wife in the flood and was overcome with grief, and the treasurer, John Dibert, was known to be dead. Seven of the 20 members of the City Council were also dead.

Arthur J. Moxham, president of the Johnson Steel Street Rails Company, was elected general chairman of the com-mittee. Captain Hart was placed in charge of the 50 special deputies. The Reverends Beale and Chapman supervised the morgues. George T. Swank, editor of the *Tribune,* and Cyrus Elder were members of the finance committee. Dr. W. E. Matthews and two colleagues were in charge of sanitation. Other committees governed the distribution of supplies, the removal of dead animals and debris, the precautionary destruction of "dangerous" buildings, the fire-fighting facilities, employment, registration and information.

A mass meeting of all the survivors able to attend was held on June 4, and dictatorial powers were given James B. Scott, chairman of the Pittsburgh Relief Committee. Scott was, in fact, designated as "dictator" of Johnstown, the word then not having fallen into its present disrepute. "Unpleasant feeling" had sprung up between the Johnstown and Pittsburgh committees, according to the New York *Herald*, but the citizens of Johnstown believed Scott's dictatorship would "be an additional guarantee of fairness and impartiality in the disbursement of funds." A number of people feared that the city's industries would be given a disproportionate share of the relief funds for their own rehabilitation, with other reconstruction taking second place. Moxham resigned as chairman of the local committees the next day, announcing his belief that "it was good policy for himself and other manufacturers and tradesmen to shape their affairs as rapidly as possible toward resumption of business."

"Dictator" Scott himself was superseded on June 12 by Adjutant General Hastings, with the 14th Infantry under his command. The militia regiment remained in Johnstown until July 13, when all but one company was withdrawn. Its only casualty was a private in Company C, who used his rifle to blow out his brains, apparently because of some private difficulty.

The militia conducted itself with such exemplary discipline that George Gibbs of the *Tribune* wrote, "The soldiers came, their rows of white tents standing where the Second Ward used to be, and the boys were ready for any hardship if only they could serve, guard and protect us. Seeing them, the mind went back to the carnage of our Civil War, and we thought of great armies cutting each other to pieces when the battle was on, then offering certain aid and comfort to the wounded of the vanquished enemy. How differently nature behaves when she has done her worst! Pitiless, unrelenting, she pursues and threatens with pestilence those who may survive her assaults, heaps horror on horror, and says to weak and strong alike, 'Obey my laws or pay the penalty.' Bless the soldiers, with their human hearts!"

General Hastings' only difficulty with the militia was a certain amount of overeagerness, which he was not disposed to view with a kindly eye. A reporter described the unauthorized arrival of Battery B from Pittsburgh.

"Who sent you here?" demanded General Hastings.

The battery commander, Lieutenant Sheppard, expected to be welcomed with huzzas. "I was sent here by the Chamber of Commerce," he proudly replied.

"You have committed a serious breach of discipline," said General Hastings, "and my advice to you is to get back to Pittsburgh as soon as possible, or you will be mustered out of the service."

Guns and all, the dispirited battery took the first train home.

The greatest physical problem confronting the relief authorities was how to dispose of the hummocks of debris behind the Stone Bridge. Until a path was dug or blasted through the wreckage, the water backed up over the river flats could not flow freely down the Conemaugh valley, nor could the bodies of humans and animals be removed. It would be impossible to control disease until the wreckage and its corruption were cleared away. Then the rivers themselves would act as cleansing agents. Yet there was bitter controversy over putting out the fire in the ruins. The survivors wanted the flames extinguished so the bodies of their dead could be recovered. Medical men, on the other hand, wanted the fire to burn itself out as a sanitation measure. The New York *Times* quoted one physician as saying, "It would be better to permit nature's greatest scavenger—the flames—to pursue their work unmolested than to further the decay of the bodies." But, the *Times* man reported, the "warnings of science were lost upon those who sought the remains of those near and dear." The survivors' wishes prevailed, and most of the bodies were recovered.

Then the question was how to attack the charred and water-soaked ruins. They were bound together with 200,000 pounds of steel wire and nothing short of explosives would make the slightest impression on the more than 30 acres of tightly woven rubble.

Into this situation stepped, with all the confidence in the world, one Arthur Kirk, of Pittsburgh. He was a demolition expert who preferred to be known as the "Prince of Dynamiters." Short, sturdy and compact, Kirk had a Napoleonic turn of mind. He was one of those feisty little men who seem to swagger even when sitting down.

Kirk was a hero during his first few days in Johnstown, attacking the drift behind the Stone Bridge with energy and determination unmatched among those who had come to restore the city. He received supplies from Pittsburgh and a donation of 1,000 pounds of explosives from The Dynamite Company of New York, and on June 5 set off his first blasts. He managed to clear an area 30 by 75 feet the first day.

A New York *Sun* reporter at the scene wrote, "Dynamite added its horror to the mass of wreckage that lies above the railroad bridge. A half dozen times this afternoon the heavy thunder of the huge cartridges was heard for miles around and fragments of the debris flew high in the air, while at a distance the crowd looked on in dreadful sorrow at the thought of the additional mangling that the remains of hundreds of bodies still buried in the mass were bound to undergo. There was little complaint, however, even on the part of those who have relatives or friends buried there, for the work of the past few days had shown how futile was the idea that anything but an explosion could effectually break up and remove the compact mass. All that hundreds of men have been able to do has amounted to nothing more than a little picking around the edges."

The cleared area was increased to 100 by 300 feet by June 10, and 200 lumberjacks arrived from Michigan to attack the wreckage with their axes. Steam winches were set up on the Stone Bridge to tug away at sections loosened by the explosions. But neither brawny arms nor steam winches were particularly effective in wrenching apart the wire-bound mass. A 75-ton locomotive was unable to uproot a birch tree caught in the drift.

Dynamite in large doses was the only remedy, Kirk decided, despite the frightened protests that came from all over the valley. To dislodge a freight car jammed in the drift he nailed a 20-pound charge of dynamite to a board and lowered it into the water. A pillow case filled with 80 sticks of dynamite blasted loose a section of house wreckage tightly embraced by hundreds of feet of steel wire.

The reporters naturally found the picturesque "Prince of Dynamiters" a ready source of copy, and one of them described Kirk in action:

He personally superintends the preparation of all blasts, and when ready emits a peculiar cry, more like a wail than a warning. Then he surveys the atmosphere with the air of a major general and yells "Fire!" The yell often terrifies the spectators more than the explosion.

Many were less admiring, however, and believed he was being carried away by his own enthusiasm. He set off a 450-pound charge to loosen the drift above the Stone Bridge to The Point, 600 feet away. Up and down the valley windows were broken, walls were shaken, plates danced on tables, plaster came tumbling down. Alarmists said Kirk would blow up what the flood had left standing.

On June 12, however, the "Prince of Dynamiters" was deposed and the state took over the job of clearing the river channels. Major W. M. Phillips, in charge of the demolition, was much less colorful than Arthur Kirk, but some of his effects were just as spectacular. He exploded 400- and 500-pound charges of dynamite, often late at night, tumbling people out of their beds. Chimneys were knocked down and water mains were broken by the explosions. Railroad ties erupted from the wreckage and plummeted through the roof of the Cambria Iron Company. Public indignation rose to such a pitch that the arrest of Major Phillips and his assistants was demanded.

While all this dynamiting was going on, 5,000 workmen were imported from Philadelphia and Pittsburgh to clear away the muck and debris in the streets beyond the drift. Not entirely attracted to Johnstown by humane impulses, they staged a sitdown strike on June 20 until their wages were increased from $1.50 to $2 a day. They had some cause for complaint, since the contractors for whom they worked were taking out 50 cents a day for food. The rations of "fat pork and black coffee" were thereupon improved, and the men took up their shovels again.

A channel from the bridge to The Point was finally cleared

on June 26, and Major Phillips began using coal oil instead of dynamite to reduce the size of the drift. On July 9 Kirk, somewhat less princely, returned to Johnstown and replaced Major Phillips, who was needed elsewhere.

This time Kirk was more conservative in his methods, using smaller charges and promising he would use explosives only between 8 A.M. and 7 P.M. Even so, it was hard to sleep, most survivors found. From 7 P.M. until dawn Kirk set fire to sections of the drift, and the people were awakened by the lurid reflection of the flames dancing on their walls and windows. The blasting and burning continued until late in August. Finally, on August 22, the Little Conemaugh and the Stonycreek were completely clear of obstruction, and flowed unvexed down the Conemaugh valley.

Among the first technicians to descend on Johnstown after the flood were 125 morticians, and the services of every last one of them were urgently required. In the following weeks, 441 of the identified dead were buried at Grandview cemetery and 115 in the public plot in another part of the cemetery; several hundred others were interred in the Sandyvale, Old Catholic, German Catholic, Lower Yoder and St. Mary's cemeteries, and a number of others in cemeteries elsewhere in Pennsylvania and the eastern states. A rather startling total of 967 persons was listed as "not known to be found."

Before all these lists could be neatly drawn up, there was the wretched process of recovering the bodies, laying them out in rows in the various temporary morgues, waiting for them to be identified by the throngs of people who passed through every hour of the day and the night, seeking a familiar face and form, dreading to find it, yet receiving some comfort out of a hasty but decent burial for their relatives or friends. To speed the process of identification eight morgues were established in Johnstown, one at Ninevah, where so many bodies were recovered from the river, and another at Blairsville. As soon as the bodies were identified they were wrapped in shrouds and buried immediately. Those not immediately identified were kept two days and then interred, but records were kept of each victim's clothing, jewelry, dental work, and possessions.

Among the hundreds who filed past the rows of bodies in the Adams street schoolhouse was William Ocher, of Philadelphia, who was seeking his fiancée. Ocher had started for Johnstown as soon as he heard of the flood, knowing that his fiancée, Carrie Diehl, of Shippensburg, was visiting her friend Jennie Wells, a young teacher in the Johnstown schools. It took him until Tuesday to reach Johnstown. The first morgue he visited was in the Adams street schoolhouse, and the second body he saw was that of his fiancée. Near by was Jennie Wells' body. Both girls had sought refuge in the Hulbert House and were among the many caught in its collapse. Ocher had both bodies placed in coffins and took them to their home town of Shippensburg the next day. The day after that they were buried.

In Alma Hall a room was set aside for various possessions found on the unidentified bodies. A partial listing of those sad relics:

Three rings "found on a female, weight 185 pounds."

Twenty-five dollars "found in a black silk stocking with the foot of a female in high button shoes."

Seven hundred and four dollars "found on a male, light hair, weight about 150 pounds."

A ring with the initials "F.M.-L.H.," found on "a woman about 55 years old, hair partly gray, dress black."

The Waters Recede

White dress and brown bib of "a girl about six months old, dark hair."

To the physicians in charge of restoring a measure of sanitation, death was viewed less sentimentally, as part of a medical problem. The dead must not be allowed to endanger the living. The Sanitary Corps, with Dr. Matthews as its chief under the direction of the state health officer, with 222 laborers and 22 inspectors, doused the whole valley with disinfectants. "The floodwater was heavily charged with every kind of filth," Dr. Matthews reported. "There was not a place that the flood touched where a man could lay his head with safety."

In the Kernville section alone, 12 wagonloads of disinfectants were spread daily. One shipment of supplies listed by Dr. Matthews, every ounce of it put to immediate use, included: 4,000 barrels of quicklime, 500 barrels of chloride of lime, 1,700 bottles of bromine, 110 barrels of Bullen's Disinfectant, 100 tons of copperas, 100 gallons of carbolic acid, three carboys of muriatic acid, 40 gallons of nitric acid, 180 barrels of rosin, 200 barrels of pine tar, 73 barrels of pitch, 100 kegs of Utopia, 15 barrels of Sanitas, ten carboys of embalming fluid, 700 bottles of Platt's chlorides, 116 pounds of corrosive sublimate, 100 bottles of Werther's Disinfectant, 100 bottles of bromo-chloralum, and $2,500 worth of Quibells Brothers' Disinfectant shipped from England. Every street and alleyway was sprinkled with disinfectants, and 1,200 cellars were cleaned out and disinfected by the Sanitary Corps. Sewer outlets along the Stonycreek river were cleared.

The result of all this vigorous campaigning by Dr. Matthews and his corps was that only one real epidemic flared up. From June 10 to July 25, 461 persons contracted typhoid fever. Of these 40 died. Not a health official in the country would have dared to hope that the toll from disease could be kept that low. . . .

Industrially and economically, too, Johnstown began to rise from the mud-covered ruins. Two days after the flood the Cambria Iron management announced that "the mills will be rebuilt immediately, and all men that can muster will report tomorrow to commence cleaning up." The Gautier division was almost a total loss—nothing left but the foundations, the rolling mill housings and parts of the heavy machinery—but a program of reconstruction was launched immediately. The mills up the valley also were flattened. The industrial revival, however, proceeded at a brisk rate.

Outside help was credited with a great deal of the impetus by George Gibbs of the *Tribune*. "Staunch friends, they were sticking close as a brother. They found the picture had not been overdrawn. The wildest imaginations had not painted the horrors in too vivid colors. Stunned for a moment by the extent of the calamity, they did not long remain idle. The strongest of us could do very little to help ourselves, but they could and did do much. What burdens they were able to lift from us they took upon themselves, and in their sustaining presence we found the first real comfort since the flood."

The railroads started digging themselves out of the wreckage the day after the flood. The Pennsylvania found that 20 miles of track in and out of Johnstown, and much of the roadbed, had been washed away; the division point at East Conemaugh was a total loss; and a total of 34 locomotives, 24 passenger cars and 561 freight cars had been hurled downstream. A number of large bridges and the stone viaduct across the Little Conemaugh had been destroyed. The

The Waters Recede

main consideration, of course, was repairing the trackage east and west of Johnstown so that relief trains could approach from both Pittsburgh and Philadelphia. The Pittsburgh division sent 1,250 workmen to clear the right of way, rebuild the roadbed and lay new track; a 1,000-foot washout near the Stone Bridge was repaired in two days, among other feats of labor and skill. Thousands of feet of trestle were thrown up by bridge-building crews. In 11 days the line between Pittsburgh and Johnstown was again operative.

The Baltimore & Ohio's problems were much simpler, since its tracks approached Johnstown from Somerset and the south along the line of the Stonycreek river. B. & O. trains resumed service into Johnstown only three days after the flood.

Both railroads offered free transportation to any flood victims with relatives or friends who would shelter them, with no limit on the distance of the journey, partly as a measure to alleviate the critical housing shortage in Johnstown.

It was a factor of critical importance in a city built in the triangle formed by the intersection of two rivers that the only bridge to survive was the Stone Bridge below The Point. Friends and relatives were cut off from each other if they lived in cross-river boroughs, and the distribution of supplies was seriously hampered. On orders from Secretary of War Redfield Proctor, the Army Engineers Corps sent three companies from Willet's Point in New York Harbor and one company from West Point to erect pontoon bridges across the Stonycreek at Franklin and Poplar streets within five days after the flood. In the depleted army of 1889, they were the only two pontoon bridges left in the military establishment.

Housing, temporary or otherwise, was a problem that did not yield so readily to solution. Fortunately the June weather was mild, for tents were the only dwellings available for most of the summer. Prefabricated houses were also imported, and Johnstown served as another proving ground for the infant industry. One type was the "Oklahoma," so named because it had been used in large numbers by people settling in that newly admitted state. The Oklahoma was a one-room, ten-by-20-foot house delivered in sections and quickly and easily assembled. Another type was the "Ready Made," a two-room house and slightly larger. A total of 310 Oklahomas and Ready Mades were hammered together, but relief officials sought a better house for family living. Contracts were finally let for 400 prefabricated houses to be set up by a Chicago firm which manufactured the "Hughes" house. These houses had two stories and four rooms. Business and professional men surviving the flood were provided with temporary quarters—first-floor storerooms with second-floor offices—on the Public Square.

The city slowly came to life as the month of June passed and the waters receded. The first church services were held June 9 in a schoolhouse, in the Pennsylvania Railroad station and on a street corner. One of these services was addressed by John Fulton, the Cambria Iron Company engineer who, years before, had warned against the frailty of the South Fork dam. Fulton, the New York *Times* reported, "created a ripple" in the congregation when he told his fellow parishioners: "I have in my possession, and I thank God for it, the report I made 14 [sic] years ago . . . that the dam was dangerous, and I was roundly abused by the men who are today hiding away." Fulton referred to the members of the South Fork Fishing and Hunting Club, all of whom had made themselves unavailable to the press and were shunning public appearances.

Even more outspoken on the subject was the Johnstown

The Waters Recede

Tribune in its first post-flood edition on June 14, which banner-lined George Gibbs' story with its memorable opening paragraph, "Well, the Reservoir came, and Johnstown went visiting. Some of us on very long visits indeed—never to come back." The lead editorial, titled "A Day Long to be Remembered," bitterly reminded the citizenry that "the thousands who were lost two weeks ago were struck as with bolts of lightning out of a sunny sky and died for no principle, gave up their lives for no cause." It continued:

> Eight miles above us in the mountains, a constant menace hanging over us, was an artificial lake known as the Reservoir. A few years ago along came the Pittsburgh club men, in all their spotlessness and glory, who wanted an exclusive resort where they might idle away the summer days. Costly, picturesque houses were built on its shores, a big hotel was erected, and, though all seemed lovely, the dudes were in a position to destroy us when the time should come. A rat caught in a trap and placed in a bucket of water would not be more helpless than we were. Pompeii, when the great volcano started, had a chance to run . . ."

The editorial concluded that Johnstown had been destroyed "through a work that should never have been built, and all the penalty on the heads of the innocent!"

On June 18, in a rather shaky hand, the clerk of the city council inscribed in the record of its meetings, "The Council of Johnstown Borough met this afternoon for the first time since the flood at 2 P.M. at the office of M. B. Stephens Esq. in Alma Hall. Thirteen members were present, seven are dead." According to that record, the council's principal action during that first post-flood meeting was to request the passenger agents of the railroads to stop running excursion trains into Johnstown.

It was a strangely somnolent body, judging from its archives. Still available in the city clerk's office is the huge, mudstained volume, recovered from the wreckage of two floods, which bears the title, "Minutes of the Borough of Johnstown, Oct. 19, 1886-April 5, 1890." Not one entry in that journal indicates that the council ever discussed the dangers presented by the dam above the city. The records of the last pre-flood meeting on May 22, 1889, showed that, with the rivers rising all around them and the dam growing shakier by the day, the councilmen were completely absorbed in an ordinance which provided a $1 fine for "any person who shall willfully suffer his horse, mare, gelding, mule, hog, goat, cow or geese to run at large." There was a weighty discussion over whether "cow" should be included.

12. The Town Counts Its Blessings

THE ENERGY and initiative of Johnstown's business and professional men in re-establishing themselves were remarkable. They were naturally a hardy lot, accustomed to almost yearly bouts with floodwater, ruined stocks and resultant bargain sales. One man went back into business a few days after the flood by setting up a barrel on Main street and selling cigars three for a dime at a brisk rate. Other merchants hammered together booths and sold whatever stock they recovered from the mud and rubble, or went into the booming souvenir trade.

Few were so fortunate in rebuilding their businesses as a young businessman named Peter Carpenter, who owned a sea-food restaurant on Franklin street, among other interests. He lived in rooms over the restaurant from which he was driven by the flood. When he returned the day after the flood, he found water up to the sills of his windows on the second floor. Floating on the water was his wallet containing $1800. When the waters receded, he found his moneybag containing $56 and another $13 in his cash drawer, all water-soaked but negotiable. Carpenter was able to re-establish himself in business without public or private assistance.

One week after the flood that form of organized optimism, later to be known as local boosterism, had revived and was being given utterance. Its spokesman was James McMillen, president of the First National and the Johnstown Savings banks, who told the Philadelphia *Press* that the flood actually had been good for business. "It will bring outside capital to Johnstown and a real estate boom is bound to follow in the wake of destruction. All the people want is an assurance that the banks are safe and will open up for business at once. With that feeling, they have started to work with a vim."

McMillen had reasons for sounding optimistic. Both of his banks were solvent and able to open their doors immediately after the muck blocking their entrances was cleared away. Not so the rival John Dibert & Company bank, which suspended operations with the death of its founder: it paid off 35 cents on the dollar immediately and the balance within a year as its loans were repaid. McMillen couldn't help crowing a little to the Philadelphia *Press* correspondent, although it may have sounded a little callous in cold print. "Since we first began business," he explained, "we have refused to make loans to parties on property where the lot itself would not be of sufficient value to idemnify us against loss in case of destruction of the building. If a man owned a lot worth $2,000 and had on it a building worth $100,000 we would refuse to loan more than $2,000 on the property." It was a form of conservatism that failed to survive the nineteenth century, much to the regret of millions in 1929.

Three weeks after the flood General Hastings decreed that business and professional men should erect temporary stores and offices around the four sides of the public square, now known as Central Park. The makers of the Hughes prefabricated houses were engaged to build the temporary quarters. Lots were drawn for the various locations, and by the

The Town Counts Its Blessings

Fourth of July most of the merchants were back in business.

The return of certain luxuries heartened residents who were growing weary of the staples dispensed by various relief agencies. Ice cream, strawberries and watermelons were being hawked on the streets by the end of June. A piano tuner from out of town established himself in business early in July, and there was plenty of work restoring instruments which had survived the flood but were caked with mud. A man named Kramer was selling oysters in July—it was before the "R" month superstition sprang up—and the farmers' market at Main and Market streets was re-established at about the same time. Salt-water taffy was being dispensed from a Main street booth, and Sulka's Salon was advertising the Edison Earphone Phonograph. By August such nonessential commodities as parrots, mocking birds and canaries were on sale.

An unwelcome luxury so far as Johnstown was concerned was the South Fork Fishing and Hunting Club, which most of the people blamed for the disaster. Public opinion was so strongly opposed to the club and its membership, and the disappearance of the lake was so great a blight on the scenic and recreational attractions of the place, that the club simply disbanded and its members set about trying to forget it ever existed. Perhaps the club was blamed over much; certainly the Commonwealth of Pennsylvania and the Pennsylvania Railroad shared in the responsibility to some extent, but the wealthy clubmen formed a smaller and more convenient target. The communal spleen was given vitriolic expression by Isaac G. Reed, a local poet, who wrote:

> An hour of flood, a night of flame,
> A week of woe without a name,

Johnstown

A week when sleep with hope had fled,
While misery hunted for its dead;
A week of corpses by the mile,
A long, long week without a smile,
A week whose tale no tongue can tell,
A week without a parallel!

All the horrors that hell could wish,
Such was the price that was paid for—fish.

The Pittsburgh *Commercial-Gazette* was almost alone in trying to defend the clubmen against what it called the "abuse freely showered upon them by the outside press." J. J. McLaurin of the Harrisburg *Telegraph* expressed the majority view that "50,000 lives in Pennsylvania were jeopardized for eight years that a club of rich pleasure-seekers might fish and sail and revel in luxurious ease during the hot months."

Neither the press nor the public was especially pleased by the disclosure that contributions to flood relief funds from Henry Clay Frick and A. W. Mellon, plus that of an Andrew Carnegie factory totaled only $7,000.

The New York *Times* editorialized that the South Fork Fishing and Hunting Club was "indifferent to the fears of the dwellers in the valley. It is a principle of law that if loss of property is caused by the negligence of any person, that person is legally responsible for the loss. If life is destroyed through the culpable negligence of any person, that person is liable for manslaughter. If that club of wealthy Pittsburghers is indeed legally responsible for the disaster . . . how fearful is that responsibility!" A few days before that the *Times* editorially questioned the wisdom of building the Quaker Bridge dam to enclose the Croton Lake reservoir, one of the chief sources of New York's water supply, pointing out that the lake would be 16 miles long and 165 feet deep at the lower end. On second thought, the *Times* observed that the Croton dam would be constructed entirely of masonry and designed to be twice as strong as necessary under any possible combination of circumstances. Thus far, the *Times'* fears have proved groundless.

The Philadelphia *Inquirer* expressed the opinion that "there is a very righteous public indignation directed against those concerned in maintaining that lake for pleasure purposes."

General Hastings, speaking more or less officially, remarked that allowing the dam to deteriorate to the point that it could be swept away after a heavy rainstorm was "a piece of carelessness, I might say criminal negligence."

Public indignation continued to rise when the coroner of Westmoreland county conducted an inquest on the bodies recovered from the river at Ninevah. The coroner's jury held the club responsible for "gross, if not criminal, negligence and carelessness in making repairs from time to time." Newspaper correspondents reported that the somewhat superfluous inquest at Ninevah would be used as the basis of legal proceedings against the club.

The club grounds were deserted and forlorn above the muddy gash of the lakebed as the time passed for the first families to exercise their privileges on the property. "No one will admit his membership in the club," a reporter wired his paper. "Even the owners of the cottages on the banks of the lake deny any interest in the Club. They are awaiting legal action which will probably be taken against them, and the cottages are unoccupied." The lakeside cottages were broken into and their furniture smashed, the New York *World* reported, several days after the flood.

Colonel Unger, the club president, and Boyer, its superintendent, were reported in danger of their lives, although no physical violence ever was attempted against any members of the club. A New York *Sun* reporter interviewed two men who spent the Thursday night following the flood at the clubhouse and were told by "a member of the club," probably Colonel Unger, "Gentlemen, I take no responsibility for your safety here tonight. I think I ought to tell you that I have reason to believe this place may be blown up before morning. I have information that a gang of men at Johnstown are determined to destroy all that is left of the club's property." The guests slept with windows open so they could jump out in case of an explosion, but their sleep was not disturbed.

Both the New York *Herald* and the New York *World* assigned reporters to seek out the club members in Pittsburgh, but their most persistent efforts were rebuffed for days.

The *World* suggested a "conspiracy of silence" had been decreed by the club members, none of whom would consent to be interviewed by the press.

Finally the *Herald* man smoked out a couple of the clubmen, L. Clarke and J. H. Willock, at the offices of James H. Reed, a member of the prominent law firm of Knox & Reed, and himself a member of the club. Clarke and Willock advanced the curious theory that Johnstown was "flooded by the water from another reservoir, at Lilly Station, eight miles above South Fork." Clarke remarked that it was "implausible" that their little lake could have caused all that damage. The meeting in Reed's office was held shortly after "a prominent criminal lawyer practicing at the Allegheny County bar" told the newspapers, "I predict there will be legal suits with possible criminal indictments as the result of this catastrophe."

To counteract the almost unanimously adverse public

opinion, the club membership held a meeting in Pittsburgh on June 11. The purpose, the New York *World* reported, was to discuss conversion of the clubhouse into a shelter for the children orphaned by the flood. "The members were all in favor of the idea, but they concluded that the place was not suitable for such a purpose."

Next day Reed received the *World* reporter in his office and declared that the club bore no responsibility for the flooding of Johnstown. "If a person was to come to me as an attorney and want me to bring suit against the club for damages resulting from the flood, I would not do so, for there are no grounds for such a suit." The same reporter quoted another member of the club: "The cause of the great rise in the lake was the unprecedented storms in the mountains. Over that feature, of course, we had no control."

Reed may have been predisposed in his views against anyone's collecting compensation from the club, but events proved him right. Not a cent was ever levied against the club or its members for the lives lost and the property destroyed. The awe of great wealth and political and economic power seemed to have precluded any concerted action, public or private, against the Pittsburghers. Nor could the state of Pennsylvania proceed against the South Fork Fishing and Hunting Club without involving possibly itself as a co-defendant; for the state had not only built the dam but allowed its continued existence after it was proven faulty and did not require any of the subsequent owners adequately to correct those faults.

The late-Victorian public, with its love of melodrama, its preoccupation with flawless heroes and deep-dyed villains, found a wealth of material for the imagination in the Johnstown flood. Even so, it proceeded to manufacture a considerable mythology based on the disaster. So assiduous were its labors that legend still obscures much of the history of the flood.

The villains in this mythology were the "Hungarian" looters and, less outspokenly, the members of the South Fork Fishing and Hunting Club; the heroes were even more fantastic.

By all odds the favorite legend was that of a "Paul Revere" galloping down the valley of the Little Conemaugh just ahead of the flood and warning the people along the way to take to the hills before he was overtaken by the giant wave. Many accounts identified the legendary rider as a man named Daniel Peyton. The fact that no man by that name had ever lived in any of the valley towns failed to dissuade those who preferred to believe in him. One widely circulated account read:

> Mounted on a grand, big bay horse, he came riding down the pike which passes through Conemaugh to Johnstown like some angel of wrath, shouting his portentous warning: "Run for your lives to the hills! Run to the hills!"
>
> At last he completed his circuit of the city and started in search of a place of safety for himself. To the hills, he urged his noble steed. Tired out from its awful ride, the animal became slower and slower at every stride, while the water continued to come faster and faster in pursuit.
>
> Like an assassin upon the trail of its victim, it gained step by step on the intrepid rider. But the hills are in sight. Yes, he will gain them in safety. No, he is doomed; for at that moment a mighty wave, blacker and angrier than the rest, overtook horse and rider and drew both back into the outstretched arms of death.

This Paul Revere legend was given a slightly different twist by the International Sunday School Lessons. Two years after the flood Sunday School children throughout the country were solemnly informed that booze, not a flood wave, had cut down the horseman. This version read in part:

> It is said that when the great dam was breaking which brought such terrible disaster to Johnstown, Pa., a messenger was sent in good haste to warn the city of their danger, but that entering a saloon he became drunk and failed to give the warning. And the disaster came.

Historians did their best to demolish the Paul Revere legend, but it acquired such wide currency in the press—and people were so eager to believe it—that they never entirely succeeded in their work. Many people in Johnstown still believe there was such an "intrepid rider" shouting warnings in advance of the flood. Professor McMaster pointed out that such a ride was physically impossible; Reverend Beale, in his painstaking, semi-official account of the flood, went to great lengths in exposing the fallacies of the various legends; skeptics reminded anyone who would listen that the water was three to ten feet deep in Johnstown's streets even before the dam broke and made riding impossible with any earthly horse. But the legend only proliferated in the endless retelling. The Boston *Herald* suggested that certificates of identity be issued to the hordes of heroic riders staking their claims in the wake of "Daniel Peyton."

Heroic railroad engineers also were elected to the pantheon of the Johnstown flood. There was some basis for this legend, one engineer having alerted East Conemaugh and another having raced into Johnstown with whistles blowing. But so many rival claimants sprang up that it was remarked, "One is inclined to believe that the flood was preceded by a locomotive race."

Johnstown

There were hundreds of real heroes, of course, but their efforts did not have the spectacular effects of racing a horse or a locomotive ahead of the flood. Reverend Beale was inclined to salute, in particular, those who risked their lives by leaning out over the flood from their own precarious refuges and "bearing up and helping others to cling to a means of rescue. God only knows how much of this heroism was enacted . . . This was a greater heroism than that on horseback, real or imagined." Reverend Beale told the story of another authentic hero, Father Davin, pastor of the Roman Catholic Church in Cambria City. Father Davin rescued the nuns who taught in the parish school when they were besieged by high water, carrying them to the church, which was on higher ground. He also saved a number of persons by leaning from the second floor of his rectory and hauling them out of the water. He turned his church into a combination of morgue and hospital, and worked over the survivors in mud up to his knees. A frail and elderly little Irishman, he caught three men robbing a corpse on the riverbank—one of the few authenticated instances of that crime—and tried to collar them. One of the men kicked him in the side with a hobnailed boot, apparently damaging a vital organ. Desperately ill and in great pain, Father Davin was sent to Denver. He died soon afterward at the home of his sister.

A "miracle" in one of the Catholic churches was long treasured. A statue of the Virgin Mary girdled with flowers and wreaths remained upright in the flooded church among the wreck of pews and other furnishings, the only object to have escaped damage. Church authorities investigated the claims of a miracle and found that the statue had survived because its wooden pedestal kept it afloat. But people clung to their claim of a miracle; this and all the legends of heroism provided a sort of compensation for all they had endured.

Others found comfort in superstition, recalling omens and portents of disaster that had come to their attention but were ignored until it was too late. Women particularly were prone to claim they were warned of a catastrophe by dreams and shivery premonitions. People living in the mountains above the city, in an atmosphere conducive to the supernatural, were fond of telling how ancient crones had rocked on their rickety porches and predicted the fate of Johnstown; of recalling that just before the dam broke they had seen small animals and birds fleeing from the valley.

Quite naturally, perhaps, this mass of legend and superstition soon overlay the factual history of the flood, clinging as stubbornly as the silt which overlay the city itself.

Another psychological facet of the flood's aftermath was the unspoken conviction of the survivors that their ordeal had conferred on them a special and unassailable dignity; the belief, perhaps, that they had been singled out for survival while so many others died. Many, in fact, had seemed to escape death by a miracle. Nothing affronted them so much as the wisecracking sign which hung in cheap restaurants, bars and poolrooms for many years after the disaster, "Don't spit on the floor. Remember the Johnstown Flood!"

They were also affronted by the catchpenny reproductions of the flood, such as the sideshow at Coney Island and the "Electrical and Scenographic Exhibit" on the boardwalk opposite the Steel Pier at Atlantic City. Gertrude Quinn, as an adult, journeyed out to Coney Island to see just how that entrepreneur would attempt to recapture the horror of the flood behind the garish canvas walls of his exhibit. She watched with indignation as the disaster was "reproduced" by sluicing a few gallons of water down on a wooden mock-up of Johnstown while the impresario hoarsely bawled out, "The dam has busted—run to the hills!" She wrote, "The impression was given that a river had risen a few feet over a town of flimsy dwellings and shanties; that a few chicken coops were floating about with some stupid people clinging to them, deserving to be drowned if they were too lazy to wade out and walk leisurely to the hill."

The more discerning were also annoyed by the mawkish poetry which the disaster inspired. Victorian versifiers were moved to take up their pens on all such occasions, and deluged editors with a volume of lachrymose poetry that almost equaled the flood itself. George Swank, the editor of the *Tribune*, protested that the flood had caused "sufficient agony" without anyone's having to read their output, and the Harrisburg *Telegraph* was even blunter in trying to discourage the poetic-minded: "The Johnstown poetry fiend has tuned his lyre. Get the gun! This thing must be stopped before it commences."

The flood left an indelible impression on the minds of children, who may have found the sudden disaster which wrecked their homes incomprehensible but remembered its details more vividly than any adults. Two of the most graphic accounts of the flood were written later by Dr. Victor Heiser in his autobiography and Gertrude Quinn Slattery in the memoir she produced for her own children. Dr. Heiser was 16 at the time, Gertrude less than half that old.

It was the fate of the children, particularly the orphans, which gripped the nation's sympathy most strongly. Two young women representatives of the Children's Aid Society of Pennsylvania came from Philadelphia shortly after the flood and took charge of finding homes for them. Only a few days after they set up their bureau in Johnstown the young ladies reported that "there are not enough orphans to go around, for we have letters and telegrams from all the states and only 49 orphans left." Adoption laws being much less strict then, many orphans were given homes without any legal formality. A fund was established through a Philadelphia trust company through which $50 was paid annually to the guardian of each orphan until he reached the age of 16.

Victor Heiser and many other young victims survived the experience with flying colors. Heiser was appointed director of health for the Philippine Islands 14 years later and was eventually credited with saving 2,000,000 lives as a public health officer and plague-fighter all over the world. "No man," it was said of his work with the Rockefeller Foundation, "has done more to relieve human suffering."

Gertrude Quinn, who married a Wilkes-Barre attorney, published her recollections of the flood of '89 just before the flood of 1936 revived all the unpleasant memories of the earlier disaster.

Dix Tittle, the boy who was disappointed because his father took the family to a hilltop while his friends frolicked in the flooded streets, became an official of a New York philanthropic organization. Wilson T. M. Beale, one of the sons of Reverend Beale, recently retired as the pastor of a church in Flushing, Queens, New York, and celebrated his 80th birthday with the clearest recollection of everything that happened to him and his family that afternoon 68 years ago. Ross E. Willis, who was three years old when his mother took him to visit her relatives in Johnstown in the spring of 1889, and who survived two days in an attic without heat, food or water, is director of a machine company at West Homestead, Pennsylvania.

Mrs. John Fenn somehow survived the loss of her husband

and seven children. Several weeks after the flood she gave birth to a daughter, Rachel Faith, but the child died a short time later. A long and lonely life stretched in front of Mrs. Fenn. She lived to be 84 years old.

Dr. John Richard Taylor, the grandson of a President, who performed the emergency operations for the Philadelphia Red Cross unit, recently celebrated his 100th birthday in a Brooklyn nursing home. "I did whatever had to be done," is all he will say of his heroic labors in the surgical tent.

Adjutant General Hastings' aspirations to succeed Governor Beaver were short-circuited the year after the flood, and his capable handling of the emergency in Johnstown was rewarded by newspaper attacks in which he was charged with handing out contracts in the expectation that the contractors would "return the favor" at the Republican State Convention. Actually, he was passed over at the convention when the nominations for governor were made. The politicians, in fact, found little glory in the Johnstown emergency. Matt Quay, the Republican boss of Pennsylvania, was accused of throwing contracts for cleaning up the debris to "greedy cormorants" who "heartlessly obliterated hundreds of human corpses with dynamite and made a profitable job of it." Governor Beaver and his administration were assailed for "conducting their conferences in star-chamber fashion," and for being "so swollen with their own importance that it is impossible to get from any of them an intelligible statement."

W. Horace Rose, the attorney who barely escaped the wreckage of his house with his life, slowly mended from his injuries and two years after the flood was elected mayor of Johnstown. C. W. Heppenstall, a young man who risked his life to rescue a woman and a girl on a housetop careening down the river, became a Pittsburgh steel magnate. Maxwell McAchren, who saved Gertrude Quinn's life, for many years dropped by her father's store on the Fourth of July. James Quinn "enjoyed hearing him elaborate on his gallant deed" and "there was usually a five-dollar bill forthcoming with which Max celebrated." William H. Pickerill, the Pennsylvania Railroad telegraph operator who kept relaying warnings from his tower at Mineral Point, stayed at his job until 1922, when he retired after almost a half-century of service with the rare distinction of never having been reprimanded for an infraction of the company's rules. John G. Parke, the young engineer who warned the residents of South Fork that the dam under his supervision was about to break (and who was probably the inspiration for the "Daniel Peyton" legend), was employed as an engineer by a Pittsburgh steel company for many years. In many ways, the man who exhibited the greatest moral courage after the flood was Colonel Unger. Much of the public anger was focused on him as president of the South Fork Fishing and Hunting Club, but he refused to leave the 250-acre farm he had bought on the shore of what had been Conemaugh Lake, although none of his fellow clubmen showed their faces in the Johnstown area after May 31, 1889. He stayed there until he died in 1896, a lonely and embittered man.

The flood situation in and around Johnstown eventually was ameliorated, presumably for all time, but not before half a century of seasonal woe and misery had passed. It cost a little more than eight million dollars to provide relief from floods which had cost ten times that amount in property damage alone since Joseph Johns had founded his town at the meeting place of the Little Conemaugh and the Stonycreek. The toll in sorrow was incalculable. Even from the purely economic standpoint, it was remarkable that a rich industrial community had to wait that long for a release from the constant menace of its mountain streams.

Only two years after the disaster of 1889, the city was flooded and both the Cambria Iron Company and the Johnson Steel Street Rails Company were inundated; floodwater encroached on Main street; hundreds of homes were flooded. One faltering step forward was then taken: the channel below The Point was widened to 260 feet to allow a greater runoff of floodwater below the city. In 1894, Woodvale was half drowned when a spring storm broke suddenly and caused a six-foot rise on the Little Conemaugh, and the backwash from The Point damaged most downtown business houses below Main and Clinton streets. Two teen-agers lost their lives that year when they slipped from the embankment into the swollen river.

In 1902, a sudden thaw of the mountain snows sent the rivers toward their high-water marks again. Hundreds of homes in the lower part of the city had to be evacuated and the lower works of Cambria Iron were deluged again.

On March 14, 1907, the city was flooded worse than any other year up to that time, except for 1889, when a sudden thaw and a heavy rainstorm combined to cause an overflow of the rivers. With the example of 1889 always before them, the people were quick to evacuate and the only life lost was that of Homer Wressler, the son of a minister, who was dragged into the Little Conemaugh while trying to lasso drift logs. All of the downtown streets were covered with water; houses were carried off their foundations and debris littered the streets. The merchants sold $5,000 worth of rubber boots that afternoon but lost many thousands more in ruined merchandise.

World War I and the postwar prosperity caused by a

steady growth in the steel industries, coal and iron mining around Johnstown, with Bethlehem Steel buying up Cambria Iron and expanding its works up the river, and Lorain Steel taking over the old Johnson Steel Street Rails Company. The metropolitan population grew to over 100,000 by 1930. The steel puddlers wore silk shirts, and there was a radio in every living room, a car in every garage and a chicken in every pot, at least on Sundays; their employers collected yachts, chorus girls, castles and Rolls Royces. But the swiftly descending rivers were untamed and still capable of bringing disaster down from the summit of the Alleghenies. Virtually none of the money so freely circulating in the 'twenties could be spared to control the rivers. If occasionally people thought back to what had happened in 1889, they comforted themselves with the reminder that there was no longer a millionaires' lake squatting up in the mountains and waiting to come thundering down the valley.

This drowsy complacency was rewarded, long after the depression of the 'thirties began, by the second worst disaster in the city's history.

The winter of 1935-36 was unusually severe, weeks of sub-zero temperatures and snow covering the ground for months. In mid-March the thaw began with a rush in the heavily blanketed mountains, saturating the soil, sending rivulets down every hillside, torrents down every watercourse. All over the western watershed of the Alleghenies the rivers were overflowing. On the night of March 16 a rainstorm dumped its burden over Johnstown and the mountains which enfold it. The rivers were rising 18 inches an hour. Robert Tross, the local forecaster for the U.S. Weather Bureau, issued a flood warning. At the Franklin street bridge the Stonycreek was running 16 feet deep.

This time, at least, there was no gigantic wave suddenly

battering its way down the valley from South Fork. It was a more gradual, but quite inexorable, inundation of the city. At two o'clock in the afternoon of March 17 the Stonycreek overflowed its banks, and a short time later the Little Cone-maugh also escaped from its channel and went surging over the flats to join the Stonycreek above The Point. The rivers thus met in the heart of downtown Johnstown, and the buildings of the business district were especially hard hit. Three steel bridges were knocked out, the Franklin street and the Poplar street over the Stonycreek and the Maple avenue over the Little Conemaugh. Cambria City, below The Point, suffered heavily. In the flood of 1889 the drift behind the Stone Bridge had spared it considerable damage but there was no such artificial bulwark this time; the water in the streets of Cambria City, in fact, was a foot and a half higher in 1936 than in 1889. The downriver boroughs of Morrellville and Coopersdale were in similar straits.

Almost a third of the population was made homeless as the floodwaters poured through Johnstown that chill and rainy afternoon. Eighteen of the city's 21 wards were flooded.

The telephone, now in much wider use, was a great comfort as friends and families reassured each other that they were safe. Something of the fearful suspense of '89 was thus lacking, thanks to better communication facilities. Late in the day, however, the main telephone exchange was swamped and all the lines went dead. All day the city firemen had been trying to shore up the anti-flood defenses of the electric power plant, keep the boilers going and the lights on. This plant, too, was flooded. Johnstown was in total darkness. Its telegraph lines were washed out by nightfall.

Once again Johnstown was isolated from the world. Its

name leaped into boxcar type of newspapers all over the world. They had said it couldn't happen there again, but "Johnstown Flood" once more sent a shock wave through humanity. All night the nation and the world wondered what had happened to Johnstown behind its mountain barriers, and again a corps of reporters was sent hurrying to the scene to find out.

The night of March 17, 1936, in some ways, was a reenactment of the night of May 31, 1889. People were driven to the hills and held vigil under a drenching rain. Others had taken refuge in upper stories and attics, and all through the night listened, as an earlier generation had, to the menacing sound of water rising in the streets, the crack of a house being torn from its foundation, an occasional scream. Again the streets were full of wreckage, but many of the items of debris would have been more than passing strange to the earlier flood generation—automobiles, refrigerators, washing machines and radios.

Few people knew that night that the danger hour actually passed at 12:10 A.M. George C. Buchanan of the Johnstown Water Company had been keeping a precise log of the flood stages, and noted at that time that the water was beginning to recede. It fell rapidly during the rest of the night. The city had been spared worse damage largely because the Stonycreek reached its maximum overflow before the Little Conemaugh.

But the terrified residents were unaware of that fact. The water was flowing 14 feet high past the Public Safety Building, about five feet lower than the high-water mark of 1889, and no one could tell in the darkness that the waters were receding.

It was a gray and gruesome dawn; fifty millions' worth of property damage (compared to $17,000,000 in 1889).

River muck and filthy water covered most of the city. Twelve persons had lost their lives, and 12 other deaths were officially attributed to the flood through heart attacks, shock, exposure and suicide. A total of 77 buildings had been destroyed and another 2,925 damaged.

Most of the people were able to return to their homes, or the ground where they had stood, that morning of March 18. Even those houses still standing were bulging at the seams with mud and water, porches were torn off, garages swept away, floors warped, furniture and furnishings ruined. Sidewalks throughout the city were uprooted as if gigantic moles had been tunneling under the streets. It all looked so hopeless that up and down the streets, newly arrived newspaper correspondents noted, people could be seen weeping helplessly or trying to console each other. Most felt this was just one of many disasters that would befall those who stayed in Johnstown during the years ahead.

The worst scare of the flood came at midafternoon.

Somebody with a memory of the former disaster started the rumor that another dam in the vicinity was about to give way. Three of the four highest dams in the state are located in the mountains above Johnstown.

"Which dam?" people asked when told of the report.

The usual answer was Quemahoning. The Quemahoning dam, containing eleven and a half billion gallons of water, twice the capacity of the former South Fork reservoir, is located 18 miles south of Johnstown on the Stonycreek.

At 2:45 p.m. whistles blew and sirens shrilled the flood warning.

Once more the old cry, a sort of joke in pre-1889 Johnstown, was heard. "Run to the hills—the dam has broken!"

Few thought it was a joke this time. The streets, still knee-deep in water, were alive with people fleeing back to the hilltops. A highly irresponsible amateur radio operator broadcast a fictitious but terrifying account of how the city was about to be destroyed. The throngs on the hillsides stood for hours in the driving rain. By the time they realized no deluge was coming down the Stonycreek from the Quemahoning reservoir, one woman had died of a heart attack, several others of shock and exposure, and hundreds of others were taken ill.

The Red Cross again moved in and set up commissaries, shelters and first-aid stations. There were 9,000 homeless to be cared for and 60,000 persons to be fed in the first few days after the flood. The entire 112th Infantry, part of the 110th Infantry and a squadron of cavalry were ordered to Johnstown by the National Guard. Sightseers, this time, were immediately prohibited from entering the disaster area. The Works Progress Administration, then in its heyday, took over a large share of the cleaning-up operations, and this time nobody could say WPA workers did nothing but lean on their shovels and "boondoggle." On August 13 President Roosevelt visited the city and assured its residents that the federal government was determined to "keep you from facing those floods again," and pledged his support for an effective flood-control program in which the national, state and local governments would cooperate.

Still, as far as Johnstown was concerned, a lot of big talk was the only visible result. Next spring mud-clogged channels caused the rivers to rise alarmingly, with rain falling steadily for two days. On April 26, 1937, the populace was warned by radio to evacuate their homes, if they were located in low-lying sections, and go at once to higher ground. The WPA's temporary bridge at Franklin street was carried away; the rivers were rising at the rate of two feet an hour, and the streets and steel mills were flooded. The Quemahoning dam rumor was revived, but with less disastrous results this time. By late afternoon, however, the river levels began lowering and the crisis was safely passed, although not before two persons died of heart attacks attributed to overexertion in climbing the hills.

At least the April wetting served as a spur: plans were quickly approved for a $7,600,000 flood-control program. The eventual cost was $8,361,318.

Work started in 1938 and continued for five years under the supervision of the United States Army Engineers Corps. By November of 1943 Johnstown was pronounced flood-proof.

The channels of the Stonycreek and the Little Conemaugh were deepened and realigned and their banks paved with concrete. Now the floodwater from the mountains can run off at high speed and an overflow becomes unlikely. The project required enough concrete to pave a two-lane highway 62 miles long and the removal of almost three million cubic yards of earth and rock.

Now, when the snow thaws in the mountains and the spring rain descends with all the intensity peculiar to the region, the water they pour down the Little Conemaugh and the Stonycreek rushes through the city. The sound effects are ominous and the velocity of the water is spectacular, but both are harmless so far as the city is concerned.

Johnstown advertises itself as the "Flood-Free City," and there have been no throwbacks to the tragic occurrences of '89 and '36 to dispute the claim. A bronze plaque on the Public Safety Building marks the high-water mark of 1936, but it is a monument to the privations of the past rather than a warning for the future.

Epilogue

SIXTY-EIGHT years after Conemaugh Lake burst its bounds and descended on Johnstown, the dam it broke still stands in the high valley of South Fork Run. Except for the part torn out by the floodwaters of May 31, 1889, the remnants of the dam seem as solid and impregnable as the whole structure did more than a century ago, when it was one of the engineering marvels of its time.

Even with a light snow falling across the mountains and somewhat obscuring the harsh outlines of the broken dam, something of the horror it once invoked clings to the place. Time has hidden the dam itself from the conscious mind of the people who live in the valley of the Little Conemaugh. No markers, monuments or ceremonies mark its place. It is, in fact, hard to find. You turn off the road that climbs along the valley just before it reaches the town of South Fork. An old, brick-paved road straggles along the rim of the South Fork valley toward the mining village of St. Michael. Off the old road, screened by brush and scrub growth, are the two great flanges of the dam. It is about 100 yards from one end of the flood-torn gap to the other. Far below is the wintery trickle of South Fork Run, which courses along the bed of what once was Conemaugh Lake. Along the floor of the valley also runs a branch of the Pennsylvania Railroad, carrying long trains of coal down from the mountains.

The dam, except for the mortal wound in its middle, appears to be almost as stout as the seven-arched Stone Bridge down in Johnstown, which still bears up under the traffic of the Pennsylvania's main line. Down the dam's broad flanks can be seen the chunks of rock, almost the size of boulders, which formed its riprapping. The view from the western end of the dam is like that from the roof of an eight or ten-story building. A coal train moving along the valley floor looks like a model railroad. The dam's immensity, considering the date of its construction, is amazing. One can understand how many people could believe it would hold against any force of water. Then, glancing up the valley through the sifting snow, one must also imagine the pressure exerted by the water collected in the catch-basin of the valley, filling the artificial lake from one steep flank to the other. Then even that massive barrier of earth and rock seems flimsy by comparison. Then, too, it may be imagined what a deafening roar must have accompanied the flood tide as it plunged down the valley.

Farther up the road the old clubhouse of the South Fork Fishing and Hunting Club still stands, sadly deteriorated since the days when the Pittsburgh millionaires and their ladies surveyed the placid lake from its wide veranda. The three stories of what is now called Clement's Hotel are ramshackle and weathered to a dingy gray. It is difficult, if not impossible, to imagine the strum of a mandolin drifting up the lake shore from the canoe of a white-flanneled stripling and his girl in summer muslin.

Yet it was on this veranda that the gentlemen from Pittsburgh rocked in their chairs and occasionally considered the matter of adequately repairing the dam. Considered it, decided against it, and one day heard that their beautiful lake had shot down the valley and taken more than 2,200 lives.

Acknowledgments and Bibliography

IN THE research and preparation for this book, the author became indebted to scores of persons who offered their recollections of the Johnstown flood and those of their families. Regrettably they are too numerous to be listed here.

Considerable assistance was also rendered by Ben Coll, day managing editor of the Johnstown *Tribune-Democrat*, who made available his own great knowledge of the disaster and the resources of his newspaper, particularly the reference library and files. Also of great help were the City Clerk's Office of Johnstown and the staff of the Cambria Free Library in Johnstown.

Sylvester Vigilante of the New-York Historical Society was, as always, a fund of information and inspiration; likewise Pete Campbell of the New York *Journal-American's* reference room, and the staffs of the New York Public Library's newspaper division, the Library of Congress, the New York and Philadelphia public libraries.

The author is especially indebted to the Historical Society of Pennsylvania in Philadelphia for access to the manuscript of John B. McMaster's semi-official report on the disaster compiled for the Flood Relief Commission.

Following is a selected bibliography:

Johnstown

BOOKS

Alexander, Edwin P., *The Pennsylvania Railroad*, New York, 1947.

Andrews, J. Cutler, *Pittsburgh's Post-Gazette*, Boston, 1936.

Beale, The Reverend David J., *Through the Johnstown Flood*, Philadelphia, 1889.

Biographical and Portrait Cyclopedia of Cambria County, Philadelphia, 1896.

Chapman, The Reverend H. L., *Memoirs of an Itinerant*, privately published, no publisher or date of publication listed.

Connelly, Frank and Jenks, George C., *Official History of the Johnstown Flood*, Pittsburgh, 1889.

Dieck, Herman, *The Johnstown Flood*, Philadelphia, 1889.

Downey, Fairfax, *Richard Harding Davis: His Story*, New York, 1933.

Field, The Reverend C. N., *After the Flood*, Philadelphia, 1889.

Gramling, Oliver, *AP: The Story of News*, New York, 1940.

Heiser, Victor, M.D., *An American Doctor's Odyssey*, New York, 1936.

Johnson, Willis Fletcher, *History of the Johnstown Flood*, Philadelphia, 1889.

McLaurin, J. J., *The Story of Johnstown*, Harrisburg, 1889.

O'Brien, Frank M., *The Story of The Sun*, New York, 1918.

Ross, Ishbel, *Angel of the Battlefield*, New York, 1956.

Slattery, Gertrude Quinn, *Johnstown and Its Flood*, Wilkes-Barre, 1936.

Swetnam, George, *Pittsylvania Country*, New York, 1951.

Walker, James H., *The Johnstown Horror*, Chicago, 1889.

Works Progress Administration, *The Floods of Johnstown*, Johnstown, 1939.

Acknowledgments and Bibliography

Works Progress Administration, *Pennsylvania Cavalcade*, Philadelphia, 1942.

MAGAZINES

Pennsylvania Magazine of Biography and History (which contains most of John B. McMaster's report in its issues of July and October, 1933)
Harper's Weekly
American Legion Magazine
Wide World Magazine
Western Pennsylvania Historical Magazine
Engineering News & American Railway Journal
Leslie's Weekly

NEWSPAPERS

New York *Times*
New York *Sun*
New York *Herald*
New York *Morning World*
New York *Evening Post*
New York *Journal*
New York *Tribune*
Philadelphia *Press*
Philadelphia *Public Ledger*
Philadelphia *Evening Telegraph*
Philadelphia *Record*
Philadelphia *Sunday Mercury*
Pittsburgh *Commercial-Gazette*
Pittsburgh *Post*
Pittsburgh *Sun*
Harrisburg *Telegram*
Johnstown *Tribune*

182